THE
SAT READING
EPIDEMIC

FORTHCOMING BY TUTOR JACOB

THE SAT MATH EPIDEMIC

THE SAT WRITING EPIDEMIC

THE ACT SCIENCE EPIDEMIC

THE SAT
READING
EPIDEMIC

JACOB BIGHAM
OF TUTORJACOB.COM

10 9 8 7 6 5 4 3 2 1

To all my students

TABLE OF CONTENTS

INTRODUCTION

Aren't There Already a Million SAT Guides?!

Tutors and teachers and prep books, oh my! These days, it seems that the only thing more ubiquitous than SAT prep is Donald Trump's Twitter stream—and even then SAT prep is a very close second. You've got your free-for-all options like Khan Academy, your luxury-brand options like Kaplan's "master tutors," and everything in between. The test prep aisle of any bookstore stretches from wall to wall, and much of that real estate is dedicated to just the SAT. Every year, students consume these products and services in increasingly jaw-dropping numbers. Still, while publishers always release new editions of prep books, and tutors and test centers continually hike their prices, their approaches remain the exact same: practice test, practice test, practice test.

Oh, you ran out of time? Try another practice test and see if you have enough time then. You're bad at trig problems? Oh, okay, look at this equation sheet and then take another practice test. Oh, that exam was actually a bad test with lots of mistakes and typos? Try this other practice test instead. You struggle with questions that ask you to state an author's main idea? I see. Have you considered trying another practice test? I'll show you how to do this one problem that you missed, so when you take another practice test—which, of course, won't have this exact problem on it—you'll need to come back to me with even more questions, followed by a practice test.

Sound familiar? I know. It pains me, too. The problem with this approach is that the vicious cycle of taking practice tests and reviewing wrong answers does next to nothing to change your cognitive processes. It's one thing to see the correct answer and, with the knowledge that it is indeed correct, craft an argument for it. It's an entirely different beast to build your understanding from the ground up and develop your skills, especially when you hardly ever practice analysis at school.

Studying for the SAT is like studying for an interview. If I were to ask you, "What's your greatest weakness?" you could easily prepare and rehearse a response to that question. Maybe you interviewed for yearbook or leadership back in freshman year, and when they asked you that question, you totally bombed. No problem. You reasonably decided to keep your chin up and prepare for your next opportunity. You went back and thought of all the questions you flubbed on and got your prepared answers in tip-top, no-one-could-possibly-turn-me-down shape.

So, when next year you decided to interview for (insert extracurricular your school offers here), you were totally prepared for every "What's your greatest weakness?" and "Tell us about yourself" they could hurl at you. They started you off easy as predicted: "So, tell us a little bit about yourself." Cool. You practiced that one. Then came a few more softballs. No problem. But then, from out of nowhere, came a question you'd never prepared for: "Upwards of 20% of Americans cannot find the US on a globe. What do you think is responsible for this?"

Uh oh! No canned response for that one. If you're anything like Miss Teen South Carolina in 2007, you might have responded with something along the lines of

I personally believe that U.S. Americans are unable to do so because, uh, some people out there in our nation don't have maps and, uh, I believe that our education, like such as in South Africa and, uh, the Iraq everywhere like such as and I believe that they should our

education over here in the U.S. should help the U.S., er, should help South Africa and should help the Iraq and the Asian countries so we will be able to build up our future for our children.

Twelve years later and it's still one of the cringiest videos I've ever watched. If you haven't experienced it already, you can find the video by searching for "I personally believe" on Google—not even YouTube. Just Google. At first glance it may seem as though she was unprepared for the Q&A round of the beauty pageant, but that's absolutely not the case. In fact, she was too prepared, to the point of rigidity. In all of her practice, she probably began her answers with "I personally believe," and to sound smart she used "such as" wherever possible, likely always closing with the perennially-clinching "to build up a better future for our children." If anything, she probably did everything her coach told her to do and say, exactly as rehearsed.

Her problem—and this is also the problem with the current meta of SAT prep—was that she prepared for old questions: if the judges had asked her any questions from old pageants, she probably would have nailed them. Instead, with her rudimentary, bits-and-pieces conception of what makes a good interview response, she was bested by variety. (She'd have fared much better had she instead practiced public speaking and interviewing, watched videos of herself, and then practiced her weaknesses even more: Do I tend to repeat phrases? Do I take enough time to pause and reflect before I answer questions? Do I seem genuine? Do I know what a map is?)

By preparing for future problems exclusively by solving past ones, she made a crucial error that we all often make as well. Should, on a quiz, I forget what 7 X 12 is, I can just memorize the product and more or less never miss that question again. Awesome. However, if later another test asks me what 7 X 19 is—and I never learned multiplication proper—then I'm at a complete loss, and I'll have to guess. But never fear! Now I'll just memorize the product of 7 and 19 and never miss it again. Then another test asks me to multiply 7 and 32, and so on…[1]

Certainly, this type of preparation works extremely well for your times tables, DMV exam, or citizenship test, where there's a limited set of possible questions and the answers are always identical.[2] For any other assessment, though, memorization simply doesn't cut it. If you don't build your skills and sharpen your critical thinking abilities, then no matter how many practice SATs you take, you'll likely never improve. Answering old questions correctly is not a skill; it's just a boring way to waste your time and make you feel like you're "stuck" with your current score.

Despite this obvious truth, SAT prep remains stagnant and mostly ineffective. I've watched SAT teachers who "teach" by looking over keys, pointing to evidence, and saying, "See, the answer is right there!" Some students, of course, recognize these failed practices but are locked into classes that their parents already paid for. Other students don't even realize that their instructors are mediocre; these students are convinced that they themselves are to blame—that if they were just smarter, then all the explanations would suddenly make sense. Students don't need someone to hold their hands and read answers to them. Students need to learn how to independently identify their weaknesses, develop study habits and skills to target those weaknesses, and build confidence.

Why hasn't the world of SAT prep evolved to meet students' real needs? I think one part of the reason is that the education system that produces many of our teachers and tutors is utterly ineffective, and understanding this problem is a crucial prerequisite to improving your score. Another part is that it's easier for teachers, tutors, and especially

---

1 I'm reminded of the episode of *SpongeBob SquarePants* in which SpongeBob forgets his own name because he only remembers information related to fine dining: "What's that name?! Gotta find that name!"

2 It also works exceptionally well at keeping you alive: It hurt when I touched that hot thing, so I won't do that again! I got really sick when I ate those strawberries, so I probably shouldn't make that mistake a second time.

prep book authors (who in text cannot adapt to your learning style and figure out what skills to target) to just answer old SAT questions or, worse, just write their own. The SAT, after all, isn't a difficult exam, and if teachers have the answer keys right in front of them, it's impossible for them to be wrong. Having to consider a student's needs and then to form a holistic view of that student's understanding takes far more effort. Even tougher is developing a practice regimen to meet those needs. Predictably, hardly anyone is willing to do it, most students included.

Furthermore, students are held back by the pervasive test prep myth that the SAT doesn't test your intelligence, critical thinking skills, or analytical abilities. Many students have been told that the SAT simply assesses how well they know the SAT. That's a lie, and it permits excuses like "I only got a low score because I couldn't afford a tutor" and "If my parents were rich and could pay for SAT classes, I would have scored higher." No. The SAT tests how well you're able to analyze author's arguments, apply vocabulary in context, and critically engage with texts. These are skills, and they're not endemic to the SAT. Every other SAT guide that I've read advertises "tricks" that'll help you "crack" the exam. That's hogwash. If you want to succeed on the SAT and in your college courses, then you need to develop your reading and analysis skills.

So, the question "Aren't there already a million SAT guides?" is an important and revealing one. In a sense, there really aren't—at least none that I think works... until now! In my years as a professional SAT tutor, I've found that if students really want to improve, then they need far more than for me to just explain wrong answers to them. They also need a skilled conversation partner to ask critical questions about texts and current events. They also need a life coach to guide them through the pitfalls and anxieties that come with navigating the SAT, classwork, extracurriculars, family life, and the litany of other problems that high schoolers all face. They need someone to reveal to them that they have what it takes to succeed—that their weaknesses aren't permanent and aren't their faults.

That's what this book is: one part critical thinker, one part life coach, one part skills teacher, and zero parts practice test. With this book, there's nothing holding you back from a perfect score except dedication.

I think that the chapter titles are rather self-explanatory, but before we dive into the official Arabic numeral-numbered chapters, I want to nevertheless give you a brief overview of where this book will take you on your SAT prep journey:

In Chapter One ("You're Already an SAT Master"), I explain that you already have the skills necessary to get a perfect score on the SAT (in this text, I only explore those skills germane to the reading exam). You just need to strengthen those skills. Importantly, I address how your teachers and the American public school system have restrained your critical thinking abilities.

In Chapter Two ("You're Doing It Wrong: Top Five SAT Reading Studying Pitfalls"), I identify and show you how to correct the most problematic habits and ideas that your teachers have taught you over the years. Once you've unlearned your bad habits and misconceptions—and learned a far better way to learn vocabulary—you need to figure out what skills to develop in their stead.

In Chapter Three ("What Do I Read?!"), I outline the types of texts you have to read to prepare for each passage on the reading exam. I provide you with worksheets to accompany each passage type and give you the confidence to freely explore research papers on your own. We examine how the SAT assesses your understanding of each passage type and determine the skills you need to practice while reading. Once you've built a strong foundation in critical reading, it's time to start taking practice tests. You'll still need to take them here and there; you just shouldn't use them as your primary practice tool.

In Chapter Four ("Practice Tests"), I walk you through the dos and don'ts of practice exams, how to identify wrong answers, and how to use practice exams to determine what adjustments to make to your practice regimen.

In Chapter Five ("What's It All For?"), I address some of the most common concerns that students have about their study habits, motivation, anxiety, focus, and goals. Every student runs into mental blocks and asks those "Is this even worth it?" questions, so I give you the fuel and fire to break through those barriers whenever you encounter them! If you have concerns not addressed by Chapter Four, look here.

Finally, in Chapter Six ("Memes Are Your Best Friends"), I briefly remind you that ideas are powerful—perhaps even omnipotent. Memes are at once a huge online distraction (and for some an addiction) and your ticket to a perfect score. If you want anything to change, you have to first accept that you have the power to decide what you can accomplish.

In a perfect world, every student would read these chapters in order, taking a break after each one. Of course, you can read at any pace you like, but after Chapter Two you should ideally focus on building your memory skills, confidence, and vocabulary. If you have the time, take a few weeks to exclusively develop these skills. Then read Chapter Three and spend at least a month critically engaging with texts before you wander off into the world of practice exams with Chapter Four. Consult Chapter Five and Chapter Six whenever you need a boost or want some inspiration—which very well could be right now.

If you're taking the exam very soon (say, within the next two weeks or so), then read straight through Chapter Four and, based on all the information and advice I've given you by that point, find a study schedule that works for you. You're nearing adulthood, or perhaps you're already an adult who's taking the SAT for a new vocation or non-trad admission to college, so you don't need me to lay out a practice exam schedule for you. I give you the tools you need to develop your abilities, and it's your responsibility to use them. *I personally believe* that nothing can stop you from getting a perfect score on the SAT if you're willing to put in the work.

CHAPTER ONE

You're Already an SAT Master

You already have all the skills you need to get a perfect score on the SAT. In this text, I focus exclusively on the reading section of the SAT, but this truth—that you already have all the skills you'll ever need for the exam—extends to both the writing and math sections as well. Now, don't get me wrong; if you don't know the definition of a word that comes up in the answers, you're not suddenly going to know its definition now that I've revealed this information to you. I didn't say you have all the knowledge. I said you have all the skills necessary to ace the exam. Yes, right now. *But I have such a bad memory!* Wrong. *But I haven't read enough books!* That's about to change. *I'm terrible at analysis!* Hold it right there.

You mean to tell me that you, an individual of the most analytical and ingenious species to ever exist, who right now is turning simple photons of light into complex words, sentences, and conscious understanding, can't do analysis? You, a walking supercomputer whose entire existence relies on being able to analyze your environment, can't do analysis? I don't buy it for one second. Your life quite literally depends on analysis: deciding when to cross the street, when to eat, how to react to an ominous noise, or what to say to avoid conflict and court trust. That you're even able to read this sentence means in no unsure terms that you are an analytical being. Think about how unbelievably many connections and associations your brain had to make just to fluently learn English.

And yet, despite this awesome mental power, seemingly every high schooler (and many an adult) struggles on the SAT. In fact, researchers recently uncovered, in the much-publicized and rightfully maligned college admissions scandal, that one set of parents paid over $50,000 to fly in a proctor from New York to California to answer SAT questions for their daughter, who unfairly had multiple days over which to take the exam. The result? She got a 1380. A *1380*.[1] So, we all have the innate ability to perform quick and accurate analysis—indeed, our survivals depend on it. Nonetheless, the vast majority of people are unable to translate that analytical capacity to decent scores on the SAT, which, you'll recall, gauges your analytical capacity. What gives?

Unfortunately, we've all been reared by an American education system that prizes rote memorization over analysis. In other words, although we're all fundamentally capable of analysis, our teachers engage in a constant onslaught against our critical thinking abilities in favor of flashcard learning. Consider exactly what skills we've been programmed to value and develop and, more importantly, how teachers test for them.

We learn microproblems: How many apples does Vickie have left? What's the sine of this angle? When does this reaction reach equilibrium? How fast does the length of a man's shadow change as he walks past a streetlamp? Who shot James Garfield? Along the way, need we explore the research and lines of thought that led to the math and critical thinking that allow us to answer these simple questions? Of course not. We're taught that research, analysis of primary sources, and forging connections between different artificially-manufactured school subjects are best left for adults—excluding, of course, most teachers.

Moreover, there's no inherent or natural distinction between, say, economics and philosophy—or algebra and English. We've just decided that some types of memorization problems go in one textbook, while

---

1 Pro-tip: If you spend $50,000 and cheat but still only get a 1380, then you don't deserve college. *sips tea*

other types get their own separate textbooks. The name we put on each textbook's cover is irrelevant, but this nomenclature has the unfortunate consequence of siloing our brain functions into limited categories like "algebraic thinking," "philosophical thinking," and "economic thinking."

We're taught in discrete, isolated chunks: algebra is distinct from geometry, which is in turn entirely divorced from calculus, which is unrelated to chemistry, which is altogether outside the domain of history, which hardly overlaps with economics. All wrong, of course, but we learn math from C-student math majors, and we learn history from C-student history majors. This isn't a surprising consequence. We learn to apply specific and myopic modes of thought depending on the classrooms we're in or the textbooks that adorn our desks.

As an example, I remember one especially comical question my mom asked me when I was a teenager. She stormed into my room, flustered and catching her breath as if her life depended on my answering within a millisecond, and asked me, "Jake! How many thirds are in two thirds!?" She was baking a cake, and apparently the recipe called for two-thirds a cup of oil. Confoundingly, she only had a one-third-cup measuring cup, so the recipe became impossibly difficult to follow.

Even though the answer was in the question itself—indeed, my response was, "there are two third-cups in two-thirds of a cup"— and despite the fact that my mom passed algebra, she was unable to perform this extremely basic calculation. Because the problem appeared to her a culinary one, not a math one, she was totally clueless, even when the solution to her problem was as easy as dividing 2/3 by 1/3 on a calculator. We limit our abilities to solve problems when we use certain strategies or think certain ways only in specific classes. For many, once algebra class is over, everything they learned there goes out the door, until the next time they're back in algebra class.

And then, in each of those limitingly insular classes, our classwork, homework problems, and exams reward memorization above all else. When was the last time you had a project or other assignment that made you go, "Wow, I feel like I'm a lot smarter now that I've finished"? Not smarter as in "I know more facts," but smarter as in "I'm more prepared to solve problems in the future." Perhaps never. You probably know your times tables, but do you think you could explain the concept of multiplication to an English-speaking Martian? How well do you *really* understand multiplication? Maybe you remember that South Carolina was the first state to secede from the Union, but could you apply that history knowledge to resolve conflicts in your own life? How well do you *really* understand the causes of the Civil War?

We don't learn to explain phenomena or ask insightful questions. Instead, we learn to fill in blanks and regurgitate factual data. Our classes reward us for memorizing information, so we come to equate learning and memorizing. Of course, memorizing is a *part* of learning, but it only gets us so far, as we've already seen with Miss Teen South Carolina.

All told, schools have two primary deleterious effects on us. First, they "teach" us, with compounding reinforcement mechanisms, that we are either intrinsically good or intrinsically bad at each artificially-delineated school subject. Teachers consign us to self-fulfilling doubting or confident categorical identities: either "I'm bad at math" or "I'm a math god." Once we're convinced that we're either good or bad at a subject, it's hard to change our minds. Further, these identities often don't extend beyond any one subject. A student can believe he is both "not a math person" and "really good at history," despite the fact that many of the skills needed to perform well in history class are also helpful in math.

Now, did his school merely *reveal* that he was *destined* to be bad at math, or did his school *make* him bad at math? I think the latter. This begs the follow-up question: if school teaches some of us the habits and false senses of ineptitude that lead to low test performance, then is there a point beyond which we are essentially unteachable and forever doomed to our primary-school abilities? Or, instead, can we unlearn those bad habits and false identities and unleash our untapped potential? The title of this book tells you what I think.

Second, schools limit our abilities to imagine, create, explore, and take risks. Multiple-choice and fill-in-the-blank assessments circumscribe possibilities. Even English classes, which many credit for "never having just one correct answer," offer multiple-choice, plot-based reading comprehension tests and one-definition vocabulary quizzes as indignant counterevidence to this wisdom. We're taught that short-sighted, narrow-minded perspectives win the day, a miscalculation that lands many adults in boring nine-to-five jobs where they never have to critically think, just like they learned in school.

The dangerous economic and social repercussions of the American school system aside,[2] what's most relevant to our discussion is how all these shortcomings affect your SAT performance. In brief, they make you really bad at the SAT. In fact, our schools by design teach us to focus on none of the skills important for success in life or success on the SAT. They usually do the exact opposite. The SAT requires that you think critically, understand the structure of complex arguments, know how to develop strong and well-written arguments of your own, and can solve multi-step problems—all skills that you have but are taught to not use.

My goal in this book is to train you to focus on the skills that actually matter, to get you to realize that you *already have* all the skills you'll need to conquer the SAT. All you have to do is practice what your teachers have hitherto ignored: focusing on rich analysis, training your brain to quickly remember information, building confidence, and developing your capacity for critical thinking. This is, admittedly, a task easier said than done. That means we're going to have to work hard to undo all the bad habits and ideas your teachers have taught you over the years. On the other side of that work, though, exists a you who is a better thinker, writer, reader, and communicator; a you who recognizes and capitalizes on all your potential; a you who gets a perfect SAT score.

---

2 If you are interested in further exploring these ideas (and I really hope that you are), I'll give you plenty of related topical reading in *The SAT Writing Epidemic.*

Before we plow forward, I want to make explicit what I've so far only hinted at: your teachers are probably pretty bad. Yes, there are no doubt some great teachers out there, but just a small percentage of students wind up with a truly exceptional teacher. If they were all good, none would stand out. Do I think that zero teachers in America are critical thinkers or effectively teach their students to also be critical thinkers? Of course not—but a solid 90% or so are just there because they couldn't find or hold down a job in industry and because the bar for obtaining a teaching credential is outrageously low. Teachers do some of the hardest work in the world, but that doesn't mean they do good work.

Do you imagine that your teachers graduated top-of-class in university?[3] That they were involved in cutting-edge research? That they were the best and brightest? That they're enthusiastic about babysitting hormonal high schoolers for six hours a day and not getting paid nearly enough? Not even close. Again, some are good, but probably not yours, and you're only as good as your teachers. You don't suck; your teachers do.[4] For some, this is a tough pill to swallow. Your teachers are bad.

Most relevant to our quest to conquer the SAT reading exam are English teachers—but don't think I'm letting you off the hook just yet, math, science, and humanities teachers! If your English teacher were a prolific writer whose analyses were even the slightest bit revolutionary

---

3 The astute among you may here think you've caught me in a logical inconsistency: if schools just teach us bad habits, and our teachers mostly did poorly in school, then doesn't that mean that they are actually better suited to teach? The important detail here is that, while American K-12 schools are typically terrible at teaching critical thinking and analysis to students, American universities are typically tremendous at teaching critical thinking and analysis to students. Indeed, many students who struggle in K-12 schools end up performing very well in university, where deep thinking is rewarded. This is, after all, why the SAT prioritizes analysis.

4 More accurately, the public education system hamstrings most teachers by not providing them with ample resources to reach all their students. Larger class sizes and ever-shorter class periods mean that English teachers especially cannot provide the individual feedback that so strongly controls student success. That said, it's an open secret that a lot of teachers are also just pretty bad: "Those who can't... teach."

or profound, would he or she be teaching high school English? No way. How do your English classes usually go down? Your teacher gives you a book to read (one probably

You don't suck. Your teachers do.

chosen by your district, not by your teacher) and periodically quizzes you on the plot to make sure you've read, right? But of course you're a pragmatic student, so you don't actually read. Why bother? SparkNotes and Shmoop will tell you everything you need to know. Maybe you discuss the text in class—when you don't have a "reading day"—and you have to put up with other students, who think their opinions are going to move planets, while they spew out totally meaningless "analysis" and your teacher excitedly nods along.

"Yes!" your teacher exclaims, "That's exactly why the author named him George Milton! Bravo, oh favorite student of mine!" But you don't care because you don't want brownie points, and you know that that information won't help you write your essay, get a good job, or score higher on the SAT. Indeed, the only reason your teacher bothers to ask about certain information anyways is that your teacher's teachers also bothered to ask about it or because your teacher found a question on a reading guide that another teacher wrote... not because the information was actually important or helped to develop your analytical skills. Much of what you focus on in English class doesn't matter and doesn't help you build any of the skills you'll need to succeed in college or in your future jobs. Why all the waste? Just 'cause.

Then, when it comes time to write an essay, you probably write it last-minute the night before it's due, without much thought or effort, and you're able to jerry rig what at least *looks* like an essay, which your teacher skims over and draws a big "B" on—because it's easier to just pass you than to deal with angry parents and failing grades. "Well," you tell yourself, still no better able to construct a coherent argument, "pretty good for just winging it."

What has your teacher taught you in the process? First, that critically engaging with texts isn't worth your time: why read the book when you can read the summary? Second, that analysis means figuring out why an author makes a room red or names a character Dolores. And third, that "reading" means reading novels and remembering useless details. All three are totally wrong... but are pillars of high-school English.

We've tasked high-school English teachers with fostering the critical thinking abilities of our youth, and this is what we get. Again, there are some earth-shatteringly awesome teachers out there, but if you were lucky enough to have had even one or two of them, then you probably wouldn't be reading this book right now.

You go to take the SAT and find that the reading section asks you to evaluate an author's tone and relationships between ideas within a text. You're so used to identifying symbols and pretending that you did your assigned reading that you've completely neglected how to approach reading for anything more than what's on your teachers' quizzes. Do you even remember what tone is at this point? The exam is a huge departure from what you're used to, given that on the SAT you actually have to understand what you're reading.

The sad upshot is that most students walk away from the SAT feeling that their low scores are due to innate lack of ability: *I'm just not smart enough.* But, as we've already seen, nothing could be further from the truth. The reason the SAT is hard is that it makes sense, and you've spent your whole high-school English career picking apart useless details that

> *The reason the SAT is hard is that it makes sense.*

don't make sense and don't matter. You probably walked into your first English class with most or all of the analytical skills you'd ever need to get a perfect score on the SAT. Then, slowly but surely, your English teachers convinced you that it was important to focus on brainless, menial details that obscure your understanding of whole texts. How's that working out?

I hope that I've at this point convinced you that you are worth the SAT prep journey. If you have ever once told yourself you're not good enough or that your score is too low and will never improve, or that you're "just not Harvard material," then it's high time you took a good look at how you got there. Your most important thinking skills have been systematically chipped away over the past decade—and for any adults reading this, decades. But you are so much more than your teachers taught you you could be, and now's your opportunity to harness your natural abilities to think critically and interact with complex texts.

We freak out over West Nile and Zika, Ebola and HIV, but no one seems to be talking about the educational epidemic that's afflicting our students across the nation. As we move toward an economy that more than ever rewards analysis and creativity of thought, it's morally and ethically mandatory that we transform the way students learn about themselves and their abilities. The American education system has unfairly trained you to memorize data but not to understand complex ideas. Your teachers have instilled in you a number of bad habits that are holding you back from success. Now, let's unlearn these bad habits and terribly wrong ideas so that you can get a perfect score and secure the future you deserve for yourself, no matter who's ever doubted you or led you astray.

CHAPTER TWO

You're Doing It Wrong: Top Five SAT Reading Studying Pitfalls

You're probably not studying properly—and given that you bought this book, I think you already knew that. You shouldn't feel bad about it because no one ever really taught you how to use your brain to its fullest potential. Indeed, as we've already seen, the structure of most of your classes has likely taught you how to *not* use your brain to its fullest potential. Let's change that.

All those Quizlet flashcard sets that you've hoarded over the years? Delete them and bask in the extra phone memory you've now got for selfies. If you have one of those "SAT Master List 800 XL Nonpareil Gold PRO" vocab lists, then get rid of it as well. If you also have fifteen full-length practice tests waiting for you on your desk at home, then go ahead and keep them, but file them away; we'll use those later.

In this chapter, I break down the top five mistakes that students make when studying—both for the SAT and for school generally—and how to fix them. Always keep in mind that you are by default an analytical being, so there is no doubt that with consistent practice, you can sharpen all the skills you need for a perfect score. In fact, by just Page 51, you'll already be well on your way to genius-level SAT mastery! Briefly, here are the most salient and pernicious mistakes that students make:

1. Memorizing information only for exams
2. Neglecting vocabulary
3. Forgetting details and losing focus
4. Using practice exams as study tools
5. Lacking confidence

This chapter is not by any means an exhaustive list of every possible method to improve these skills, but it gives us a strong foundation that we'll build upon later. I am sensitive to the fact that students start their SAT journeys at different levels, which means that each student needs a different amount of guidance and training. To illustrate, for some students, my discussion of vocabulary in this chapter alone will suffice to transform their vocabulary learning habits. Others will need more help and advice, which will come in later chapters. In either case, the students who take away the most from this guide will be those who work smartest.

Now, don't freak if by the end of this chapter you don't feel an electric sense of transformation. You learn and transform habits gradually; trying to change everything all at once almost never leads to success. Process and apply what I give you here, and trust that when you need further guidance, I'll provide it for you. We're embarking on a journey—a marathon, not a sprint.

1. Memorizing information only for exams

The first and biggest mistake students tend to make is brute-forcing. I'll let you demonstrate right now how brute-forcing works. Try your best to memorize the following number:

418752046051859658671259

Do you have it down? Take a few minutes and see if you can really get it. Write the number out, put this book down, and come back when you're done. If you're not willing to put in at least a few minutes at this point, I can promise you now that this book is definitely not for you.

Got it? Will you remember the number in five minutes? Five days? If you're like most people, I imagine you tried to brute-force your way to memorizing the number by repetition. You got the first few numbers down easily (and if you happen to live near Quebec City, you recognize 418 as a local area code). Maybe that little string of even numbers was a gimme: 20460. Maybe you came up with a little tune or jingle to remember the numbers, or perhaps you tried to see a pattern in how each successive number relates to the one before it (4, -3, +7, -1, etc.) but realized that that actually makes it tougher to remember the sequence. Whatever the case, I am confident that you *can* brute-force your way to memorizing those numbers. If you had maybe five or ten minutes to kill, you would most likely remember the string of digits well enough that you could regurgitate it back with roughly 95% accuracy… and then you'd probably forget it in about five minutes more. (Put another way, you could remember it well enough to get an A on an exam, but you'd forget it long before finals came along.)

This process probably sounds familiar because it's how you study: vocabulary in English, dates in history, derivatives in calculus, and molar masses in chemistry. And it needs to stop. No, really, like, we need to put an end to it right now. Bigly.

Again, your teachers have sadly convinced you that memorization and learning are one and the same—but we're in the 21st century, and your brain is capable of far, far more. Let's be real here: unless you plan to compete in trivia competitions, your ability to flourish in the 21st-century economy will depend on your ability to think fast, make complex decisions, and recognize connections between information and ideas. Doubtless, you will always have to memorize and remember new information (especially new words), but the more time you spend trying to brute-force information into your head, the less time you can invest into developing your critical thinking skills. So, the more time you put into honing your memory, the more time you'll save down the line.

Now, let's train your brain to learn things without the pain of stu**dying** you're so used to. First, I'll teach you how I would go about remembering that number from the page before last. Memory champions use a system that links together numbers and consonant sounds in order to remember lists and strings of digits. The system is so simple that anyone can learn it in just a few minutes. Each digit (0-9) corresponds to a consonant sound:

0 - S

1 - D/T

2 - N

3 - M

4 - R

5 - L

6 - J/Sh

7 - K

8 - F/V

9 - B/P

So, here's the number from before, but given as letters instead of numbers:

RTFKLNSRJSLTFLBJLFNJKTNLB

Now this I can remember because I can turn these letters into a silly story about someone I despise:

Rat! Fickle 'n' sour! Joe "Slooty Flab" Joel. Fun? Joke! Tunnel bee.

This of course sounds totally ridiculous (that's the point), and it took me about three minutes to come up with, but now I know the number. I can picture a dirty guy named Joe, whose friends call him "Slooty Flab." (What does that even mean? Who cares?) Being around him feels like being trapped in a tunnel with a huge bumble bee. What do I think of Joe Joel? He's a rat! He's fickle 'n' sour. Basically, people know him as Joe "Slooty Flab" Joel. You think he's fun? What a joke! Being with him is like being stuck in a tunnel with a bee! I can picture all these things in my head, and although it's a silly image indeed, the picture (and this is the important part) is memorable. I can't remember a long list of numbers, but I can remember that rat who's fickle 'n' sour named Joe "Slooty Flab" Joel who's so lousy that to call him fun is a joke and whose presence makes you feel like being trapped in a tunnel with a bee. Yes, that's likely a little more mental gymnastics than you might expect me to put in, but it works:

RaT, FicKLe 'N' SouR, Joe SLooTy FLaB JoeL FuN JoKe TuNneL Bee

RTFKLNSRJSLTFLBJLFNJKTNLB

418752046051859658267125

I memorized the number, and you probably did too by reading my ridiculous story about lousy old Joe "Slooty Flab" Joel. Sure, I can't recite the number on command, but give me about ten seconds and I'll piece it together. And I can do it tomorrow; I can do it next week; I can do it next year. Had I put any time into memorizing the number without a system in place, I'd invariably have forgotten it by the next page (and I'd have wasted my time). Stop brute-forcing. Use a system. Make weird mental associations. Write stories and be creative and create your own universe of characters and situations that can help you to remember whatever you need.

Not only does this make memorizing easier, but it also makes studying and reviewing easier because you're storing information in your brain by association. When you go back over this number, for example, you don't have to worry about the number itself, just the funny story you've concocted. Truly, you'll *review* information instead of flat out *relearning* information that you never really knew to begin with.

If you can remember a completely useless and randomly-generated 25-digit number in just minutes, imagine what kinds of *useful* information you can quickly and reliably commit to memory. Think of the time you'll save.

As a little practice, see if you can remember our number backwards:

9521762856958150640257814

Come up with your own clever or ridiculous mnemonic, and then return to this page in a week and see if you've still got it down.

My students find this system especially useful for remembering dates in history. When was the Stamp Act passed? Picture a stamp in jail: it's a big white stamp with an angry face, angrily shaking the bars of its jail cell in contempt of the British monarchy that has so brutishly imprisoned it. The word "jail" helps me remember that the Stamp Act was passed in 1765, since 65 is JL in our code. (There should be no need to encode the century; if you're a history student and can't remember that the Stamp Act came along in the 1700s, then all hope is lost.)

> *You have incredible untapped memory potential.*

So, how does this strategy of encoding information and visualizing stories help you to prepare for the SAT? Most obviously, honing your memory will save you a lot of time studying and a lot of heartache during exams, since it's always nice to get memory-based questions correct. More importantly, it proves that you have incredible untapped memory potential. So now, when I ask you to start reading more and to fully commit yourself to learning new vocabulary and writing styles, you cannot truthfully tell me you *can't* or that *your memory isn't good enough.* As I've said before, you're literally a walking supercomputer. Act like one.

I don't expect that you'll start using this system right away, though it would be a good idea. Learn the letter-number key so well that it's second nature to you, and you'll never again struggle with memorization! If you want to explore memory tricks some more—and there are plenty of memory tricks out there—then Google "memory pegs" or Joshua Foer's 2012 TED Talk on memory palaces.

Again, what you should take away from this section is that your memory is nothing shy of extraordinary, and you can no doubt train your memory to the point that you can quickly remember just about anything. Years of missed multiple-choice and fill-in-the-blank questions may have conditioned you to think that your memory just wasn't good— and that's true. Your memory is *great*! Train it.

2. Neglecting vocabulary

Uninstall Quizlet or Anki or anything similar. No, really, go uninstall them right now. Lose your training wheels. You're better than learning by repetition. Throw away your vocab lists. Enough is enough. No more matching or multiple-choice vocab quizzes. That's no way to learn a language: out-of-context, solitary definitions that you may or may not remember when you actually encounter a word outside the quiz. Let's do this thing right.

In honor of the alphabetized vocab list you hopefully just threw away—or, better yet, never had—let's start with one of the first words you'd likely find were you to go retrieve it from the garbage where it belongs: abstemious, which means modest, reserved, unwilling to take too much, and not gluttonous. You generally see writers use the word to describe someone who doesn't drink alcohol or devour lots of food, and it is pronounced ab-**steam**-ee-us. So, how do you remember its definition? You could, for instance, envision a middle-aged man recovering from alcoholism. He's at a bar with his friends and wants nothing more than to drink with them, but he can't because he's being abstemious. Naturally, he's so angered by his inability to drink with the other guys that steam begins to emerge from his ears. He's ab*steam*ious. Easy.

Keep a running list of words you learn, starting right now with abstemious. Write down each word's pronunciation, where you encountered the word, what it means, and a cartoon or other mnemonic to help you memorize its definition. Do not brute-force memorize vocabulary. Come up with crazy plays on words, little awkward stories that relate to the pronunciation of the word and connect to its definition. If you speak another language, see if you can make connections to any words in that language too. Of course, if you recognize any Latin, Greek, or German root(s) in a word, make note of that as well.

Make it fun! Keep a running list online with your friends and make learning new words a core part of your life. Use a British accent and incorporate more complex words into conversation with your friends (or your enemies if it'll bother them). When you're watching a show on Netflix and hear a word you're unfamiliar with, look it up and write it down. When you're reading through Shmoop and come across a word you don't know, look it up and write it down. Then, craft a funny story to go along with it. The more fanciful the story you create, the better. (If you don't know what "fanciful" means, add that to your list!) Learning new words doesn't have to be hard, and it should be fun.

I cannot emphasize this enough: expanding your vocabulary is the best way to improve your SAT score. If you don't know what a word in a passage or answer choice means, then you're screwed. There's no amount of focus or effort during the exam that can teach you the definition of a word. How many times have you, after reviewing a missed practice test question, looked up the definition to a word in an answer choice and then thought to yourself, "well, that's obviously the answer!" That's the worst feeling in the world: "I understood the passage, but I didn't know what the answer choice was saying."

But wait, how am I gonna learn new words without a vocab list... or my sweet, sweet Quizlet?!?! First off, get over Quizlet. It's just not gonna work out between you two. Second, the issue isn't finding new words to learn. Every day, you encounter dozens of words that are new or unknown to you. You hear them in school, you read them on Instagram, you see them on advertisements, and you study them for English class. You don't need someone else to curate a list of words for you. (Do you know what "curate" means?) All you need to do is to be honest and proactive about what words you know. Again, whenever and wherever you encounter a new word, learn it. Should you find that you don't often come into contact with new words, start adding a steady stream of thought-provoking podcasts to your intellectual diet. By the end of Chapter Three, you'll be reading more complex texts, which will entirely eliminate this potential problem.

> *Expanding your vocabulary is the best way to improve your SAT score.*

Don't limit your focus only to words that you haven't seen before. If you come across a word that a writer uses differently than you're used to or familiar with, then make note of it. When I see the word "patronize," I think of condescension and insensitivity: to patronize is to act supercilious, to talk down to. But in true English fashion,[1] it also means to purchase items at a store (i.e., to be a patron). I could very well

---

[1] One of the most aggravating aspects of English is that there are a million ways to say the same thing, and every word seems to have a hundred different meanings. See this as an exciting challenge, as there will always be more to learn, and you can always improve! How boring would life be if there were nothing more to discover?

patronize a store without saying anything bad about it. So, pay keen attention to the ways in which authors use words: context, connotation, and denotation are all components of a word's definition.

As a quick note, denotation means the "dictionary definition" of a word. The denotation of "mad," for example, could be "angry" or, in a different context, "insane." Connotation refers to the cultural, social, and deeper contextual meaning of a word. For instance, "mad" and "pissed off" both mean the same thing by denotation, but there's a huge difference in connotation. Some situations call for "mad," while others call for "pissed off." You need to know when to use one over the other. Proper context and an understanding of connotation are crucial components of learning vocabulary beyond just denotative definition.

Frequently, when you look up the definition of a word, you'll find that the word has multiple definitions—sometimes ones that are slang, formal, or archaic. Learn these. Vocabulary also includes idioms, like "bought the farm" and "beating a dead horse." Commit these to memory as well, since nothing is off-limits in the world of literature. A good general rule is to write down and figure out everything you don't know, whether that means single words or entire sentences.

I do recognize that that's easier said than done, and at first vocabulary seems an insurmountable obstacle. When you really start to focus on expanding your vocabulary, it'll feel like you're writing down every other word you see. You're fine. That's normal. It takes time. After a few weeks, you'll find yourself reaching for your notebook of words far less frequently—because you'll retain the words you're writing down and, of course, reviewing. Indeed, simply writing down a word and its corresponding mnemonic won't store them in your memory forever. You must consistently review.

Having a stronger vocabulary will improve your writing ability, your reading ability, and your grammar ability. You'll sound smarter, feel smarter, and be smarter... and you'll score higher!

Here's a list of my essential vocabulary rules:

1. Use a system to memorize words: stories, cartoons, and ridiculous mnemonics will help tremendously.

2. Every time you encounter a word or phrase you don't know, write it down.

3. Research how to pronounce the word, when it's appropriate to use it, and whether it has any secondary meanings.

4. Pay especially close attention to words whose meanings are radically different as different parts of speech (e.g., contingent as an adjective vs. contingent as a noun mean unrelatedly different things).

5. Be brave and persevere through the tough vocabulary times. At first, it will be extremely difficult to keep up with the maelstrom of new words, and you'll scramble to even write them all down (you really do come across a lot of new words in even a day's time). Fear not. Soon, you'll be a vocabulary master.

6. Make it fun! Tease your friends, and use a British accent: "Why, I do say you look rather pulchritudinous today, chap!"

7. Review. No matter how good your memory devices are, you'll need a refresher here and there. It's not conceding defeat to review something. Anyways, your brain remembers things way better the second and third times around.

8. Use your new words. In your writing, in your speech, and in your head, make new words a part of your day-to-day vocabulary.

Lastly, on the next page is a sample of what my vocabulary notebook looks like. Please make every effort to write down your word list on actual paper (don't keep it in the notes app on your phone). As with any memory device, the more ridiculous, outlandish, colorful, and over-the-top that you can make your vocabulary notebook, the better. It's extremely difficult to forget details that boldly stand out in memory; you remember the weird, crazy things and forget the bland, quotidian things.

smattering (n.)

- a very small amount of something
- it sounds like it means a lot of something, so remember **sma**ll **sma**ttering
- used with *of*: "he offered us a smattering of wine before dinner began"

tempestuous (adj.)

- pronounced tem PEST yoo us
- it can mean changing emotions very frequently, or it can mean windy and turbulent (of a storm)
- tempest = wind (so if you're tempestuous, your emotions change like the wind)
- think of Janna from League of Legends: she throws wind because she's "the tempest"
- makes me think of emotions that are **temp**orary

blithe (adj.)

- pronounced like writhe or lathe (soft "th" sound)
- it can mean happy or joyous, but it can also mean inappropriately disinterested
- Blithe has the biggest smile on when friends see her at a party; she's a sweet, young girl who's always cheery, but she's also **bli**nd, so sometimes she's ignorant of what goes on in her vicinity, so much so that people around her sometimes become angry
- so, if I remember the character Blithe, then I can remember the definition for the word blithe: the extremely happy and blind girl with a huge smile is a strong image that stands out in memory

This is a lot for just three words, but I will never forget these definitions. When you put in extra time upfront so your performance will improve later, that's not spending time. That's investing time.

3. Forgetting details and losing focus

Training your brain to better memorize information also affords you the invaluable ability to more accurately recall information from reading passages. Many of the questions on the reading section require you to remember key details. It terrifies me when I see that my students have finished reading a passage while I'm still halfway through—not because I feel like I'm a slow reader but because I know they're reading too fast and ignoring details. If you're going to skim, then skim. But if you want to read the passage, then don't ignore details. As I've proven to you, when you tell yourself you won't be able to remember any details by the time you finish reading—and so you might as well not pay attention to the text to begin with—you're not being truthful; you're just being lazy. Plus, why bother reading if you won't remember anything?

You might be a little confused: in Chapter One, didn't I tell you that blunt memorization is plaguing our education system? Now I want you to focus on remembering details? Also, didn't I say the SAT asks analytical questions, not memorization questions? Yes, yes, and yes. That said, you obviously can't analyze a text that you know nothing about. For example, how could you possibly determine an author's main idea if you can't remember a single detail from the passage?

Your goal isn't to try and remember a passage line-by-line so that you could recite it to a crowd the next day. It's also not your goal to memorize every detail in a passage: it probably doesn't matter what color a character's shoes are, for instance. You've likely been trained to remember textual details simply for the sake of remembering them, not because they factor into your overall appreciation for an author's argument or purpose.

Instead, when I say, "remembering details," I mean, "keeping up with the text." If you get to the second paragraph of a passage but have already forgotten a character whom the author introduced in the first paragraph, then you need to work on remembering details. If you run into a question that asks about that character, you're going to struggle.

In other words, you need to be able to pay attention and not lose focus as you're reading. We all know that feeling at the end of a page where we have no idea what just happened—which is fine every once in a while but is extremely costly on the SAT. The goal of this section is to get you on track toward staying focused on and attentive to the passages you read. When you read information, you must retain it.

Let's get into the thicket of remembering information, then. After you finish reading a passage, do you often ask yourself, "What the heck did I just read?" Are you "bad with names"? Do you find it difficult to remember phone numbers? If so, you're lying to yourself about your abilities. Your brain can perform more calculations per second than a supercomputer, and you're tellin' me you can't remember a phone number.

I just proved to you that you can easily memorize lots of information—at least with a system in place. Let that sink in: you can remember material extremely easily and accurately because you're a walking supercomputer… you just need the right programming! Part of that programming is the system I introduced to you at the beginning of this chapter (a system that, again, you need to frequently review if you really want to put it to strong use for classes at school). How does being able to memorize long strings of numbers help you to pay better attention to reading passages? It doesn't—at least not directly. It does, however, give you all the motivation you need to get over the obstacles that are holding you back from retaining passage information.

What are your obstacles? You don't know your vocabulary words, and you're distracted. If you read a passage and miss the definitions of 10% of the words, the passage becomes near impossible to follow, and you lose 100% of its meaning. You, I hope, are already working diligently to mitigate this problem by learning every new word you find, so let's address the second obstacle: you don't pay attention.

You're distracted. You don't pay attention. Your mind is lost. Part of the reason for this is that you aren't interested in much of what the SAT reading passages are saying—I address that in Chapter Five. The other part of it is that you aren't used to focusing for more than a few seconds at a time. Think about it: your mind operates in 10-second chunks. You have the focal capacity to read a tweet or an Instagram caption, but that's about it. It's not your fault. Your teachers have tacitly encouraged you to read summaries, and books take patience that most students these days have consequently not yet developed. It's okay, and we can change it.

Back in the day, people had to remember things because there were no computers—or, way back, even paper or words!—to record information on or with. When students didn't have laptops in classrooms, and they weren't distracted by Reddit and Facebook, they had the attention span to listen to their teachers for more than a few seconds at a time. When I was a kid, I knew the phone numbers of my family members, my close friends, my school, and the local pizza place. In fact, I still know most of these phone numbers. Why? Out of necessity: I either remembered the numbers or I could never call anyone. (Yes, I brute-forced back then. I wasn't prudent enough to use a clever mnemonic or even write any of the numbers down—though we did, I assure you, have paper when I was a child.)

Now that I'm older, I pretty much know just my own phone number and my mom's phone number—and even then I often forget my own. That's probably the situation for you, too, but it's not because you can't remember other phone numbers; it's because you can get by without remembering them, so you never put the time or effort into doing so. You could *if you wanted to.* Homer literally memorized the entire *Iliad* and the entire *Odyssey* with only the help of a rhythm. Ask your parents if they know Jenny Jenny's phone number (it's 867-5309). They will never, ever forget it.

If you were to meet a new friend at school and he told you his birthday, would you remember it? Would you write it down? Would you even care? Nope. Facebook or your phone or Snapchat would remind you when his birthday came along. You'd maybe send him a nice "ayyy hbd" message, and life would go on. If you forgot to send a message, it wouldn't be a big deal because birthdays aren't as special as they used to be, and there's no expectation that you'd care enough to remember, so you wouldn't. My mom, however, would be furious if I forgot her birthday because in her mind I should know it, so I do.

Okay, back to the SAT. You can remember details if you want to remember details. If someone tells you her birthday, and you make the effort to remember it, you'll remember it. Do you want a perfect score on your SAT reading section? Yes. Do you want to remember the details of the reading passages? Yes. I'm going to give you three tasks—beyond learning new vocab words—that will very quickly improve your focus and factual recall. Are you going to perform these tasks as often as you can? Yes. I believe in you!

Read an article every day.

You can't remember textual details if you don't read them first. Train your brain to focus on a text for more than just a few seconds at a time. Force yourself to sit down with a random news or magazine article every evening. Don't read an article on a screen. If you don't have access to a printed piece, then print one out yourself. Don't read an article on a screen. Train your eyes to focus long enough to stick with an author's

> *You can remember details if you want to remember details.*

argument for an extended period. Also, make sure you're pulling articles from reputable and edited sources. The SAT will pull its passages from edited and peer-reviewed sources, so you need to get comfortable with strong, academic writing. If you see typos, inappropriate language, street slang, or ridiculous arguments, then find something else to read. In Chapter Three, I discuss in great detail what you should be reading, but for now jump around and explore anything you find interesting.

Pay attention.

It's so easy these days to ignore much of what someone has to say, and a lot of that is because most information is available online anyways. Why bother wasting your precious memory on data you can store in the cloud? I'll tell you why: because doing so makes it easier to remember even more. A computer gets slower when it holds more data and its memory gets used up, but your brain gets faster when it stores more knowledge. So, when your teachers are lecturing in class, stop telling yourself you can go on Instagram because your teacher's eventually gonna post the PowerPoint. Invest your energy into listening to things the first time. You'll be amazed at how easy it actually is to remember information.

Write stuff down.

This is probably the most important one. When you write information down, you force yourself to consider that information for just a little longer (it takes a second or two to write down a phrase or a detail). The result is that you're more likely to remember something if you write it down. And, should you happen to forget that information, you've got a backup of your mental hard drive right there on paper. If you haven't practiced annotating literature, invest a bit of time into doing so. Of course, the question becomes *okay, but what do I write down?* I'll talk more about engaging with texts in Chapter Three, but for now write down anything that helps. For starters, jot down vocabulary words and information that you want to remember but know you'll forget. You also should be writing down questions when you read articles: Why did the author use this word? What is her main purpose? What was that event she referenced? Most importantly, you should write down anything you read that is weird to you. Maybe it's a word used in a new context or a sentence structure you're unfamiliar with (you can put the verb before the subject?!). If it's new to you, write it down.

I explore in Chapter Four many more ways to develop your focus, but you should start with these simple ones first. As with developing any habit or regimen, start small and then work toward more complex or time-consuming strategies. If the easy stuff works, you save time. If it doesn't, then bring in the big guns and jump to Page 94.

4. Using practice exams as study tools

Whenever a student comes to me for SAT tutoring and says she's already taken all the available official practice and released exams, I die a little inside. Practice exams are not learning tools, and if you're the type of student who thinks that SAT studying means sitting down and taking endless practice exams for hours and hours, then you are wasting time.

Students today are way too dependent on practice tests. When a teacher posts old exams or sample test questions, that tells students that they only need to know how to answer *those* questions—anything else isn't important because it won't be on the test. This kind of "learn it because it's going to get you points" mentality is dangerously stifling, fostering rote memorization instead of complex understanding. We need to reverse that trend.

That said, you absolutely should take a few practice exams if you fall into one of the following three categories:

- You've never taken an SAT before and are completely unfamiliar with the format, length, and/or content of the exam
- You've taken an SAT or two (or maybe the PSAT as a freshman or sophomore) but still don't feel all that comfortable with the format and don't have a general sense for the types of questions the exam tends to ask
- You're taking the SAT very soon and don't have much time to develop most of your strategies and reading abilities

Otherwise, stop taking those practice exams. Please. Use practice exams to track your progress over time. Take them only after you've practiced the techniques I teach you in Chapter Three and you've read Chapter Four.

By the way, there are enough official practice and released exams online that you should absolutely not waste your time or money on any practice exam materials not produced by the official SAT. You wouldn't train at baseball if you're a softball player, and you wouldn't practice rugby if you wanted to be an NFL star. The College Board spends millions of dollars to make sure their SAT exams are unambiguous and error-free.

Master your SAT skills before taking your practice exams.

I can't get through one section of most prep books without finding a dozen poorly-written questions. I want to save you time and unnecessary work. Use the real exams.

I won't go into detail here regarding how to properly use practice exams; again, I do that in Chapter Four. If you're taking the SAT in a week, then go ahead and skip to that chapter now. Otherwise, read it later. You need to master your SAT skills first, and then you can worry about taking practice exams. Please, for the love of all that is good, stop taking practice exams.

5. Lacking confidence

Ah, yes, confidence, the one thing that no one seems to have quite the right amount of. I want you to walk into your SAT feeling like you're gonna absolutely crush it—not just because I think that confidence is important and will give you a competitive edge, but also because lack of confidence is a great deal of what's holding you back right now.

Why aren't most students confident in their academic abilities? Again, our failed education system is to blame. Teachers have neither the time nor the patience to nurture the abilities of all their students. In a class of thirty students, when one student falls a little behind, the teacher can't spend a day or two just to help that one student catch up. As years go by, this problem compounds exponentially for each student.

From kindergarten through twelfth grade, teachers slowly convince too many students that they're dumb, stupid, bad at school, or bad test-takers. For many, the root cause isn't inherent lack of ability. You can easily picture a kindergartener who, because on one day he happens to not eat breakfast, has a really tough time on his spelling test. His teacher forms an implicit bias that the student is "not good at spelling" and reinforces this with "it's okay" instead of "you can do it!" The teacher leaves notes to the student's future teachers: "not a smart student but behaves in class" or "struggles with English," and this continues for the remainder of his academic career. The cycle repeats, and his identity is unfairly forged for him by happenstance.

To make matters worse, the education system tells us that if we can memorize facts, then we're smart. If we can't, then we're dumb. Of course, even when our teachers are poor communicators or present information in ways that don't match our learning styles, *we're* still to blame. If we happen to be extremely creative artists, musicians, or writers but simultaneously struggle to remember equations in math or to spell words in English, then we're still branded bad students. Fill-in-the-blank and other memory-based assessments only reinforce this further: you either know the detail or you're a poor student.

The net product is that most students truly believe they are bad at learning, when in reality they've just had the bad luck of inept teachers and a one-size-fits-all education system. Imagine that! Your teachers expect you to remember tons of information, but not a single one ever thought it was a good idea to teach you *how* to learn and study that information. If you have ever told yourself you're not good enough or that school "just isn't your thing," I'm here to tell you that you are good enough and that schools suck anyways. Throw those ill-conceived notions of inferiority out the window. You can get a perfect score on the SAT, and you can succeed in academics.

We need to set our sights high, because you know what sucks even more than the American education system? Being *good* at something. It's really, really tough to be good. If you've ever performed in front of an audience, then you know exactly what I'm talking about. When you're just good at something, you tend to rely on rote memorization and can't fall back on your skills (because your skills aren't honed). Here are a few examples to clarify this perspective for as many readers as possible:

1. During a piano recital, you forget a few notes in the melody of a song. If you're *good* at playing piano, then you'll try your best to play what you remember from muscle memory, and you'll probably tense up when you inevitably hit a wrong note. If you're *great* at piano, then you've got no problems. You may have forgotten the melody, but you're comfortable with your scales and can improvise a melodic fill to save yourself—and the audience never knows the difference.

2. When I was in sixth grade, I entered our school speech contest. The prompt that year was to describe what makes America beautiful. I had prepared (what I thought was) a pretty stellar speech about our landmarks, firefighters, and teachers; and my great-grandfather, who was a World War II prisoner of war to the Nazis. I started the speech just as I'd rehearsed, but when I began to transition into my last main point, my brain suddenly blanked. I'd completely forgotten everything I knew about my great-grandfather. In that moment, I had two choices. I could have been a *good* public speaker and taken an awkward pause, shuffled through my notecards, figured out where I'd left off, and after a cringeworthy six or seven seconds delivered my spiel on great-grandpa Larson. And I'd have absolutely lost.

Instead, I was a *great* public speaker. I was confident in my ability to speak in strong, clear, extemporaneous sentences, and I made up a new paragraph on-the-spot… and I won! I asked one of the judges afterward why they had picked me even though I forgot what I had written down, and he told me that that was precisely why they chose me. They knew I'd messed up, but I fixed the mistake in one second instead of ten. Miss Teen South Carolina, take notes!

3. You ever watch those people on *America's Got Talent* who juggle fire and chainsaws while they're balancing on top of a ladder that's standing on a unicycle that's bouncing precariously on a trampoline? If they were *good*, they'd be dead. They've put in thousands upon thousands of hours of training and practice to make absolutely sure that when they go out on stage, they'll be able to safely handle any mishap. They are *great* at what they do, and they know it. For them, the slightest hesitation or lapse in confidence almost certainly spells disaster. So, they don't hesitate, they don't lose confidence—and they're tremendously entertaining and successful for it.

The moral of the story is that you understand the dangers and pitfalls of mediocrity. I don't want you to be a *good* test-taker and set your sights on getting a good score. That leads to underperformance, and you're so much better than that! I want you to be a *great* test-taker who knows without a doubt you're going to get a great score on the SAT!

I do want to add a disclaimer here: if you're scoring 200 on the SAT reading section today, confidence alone isn't going to get you to 400 tomorrow—or any time soon for that matter. Confidence will, however, save you time and can alone boost your score upwards of 50 points with the right applications.

How do we go about building your confidence, then? Well, for starters, I need you to accept this deep down in your bones as the truest truth you could possibly know: the SAT is really easy. There, I said it!

Especially compared to a lot of the exams you've probably taken in school or will take in college, the SAT is an absolute joke. If you don't believe me, that's not fine. I need you to believe me. I want you to literally say out loud, right now, twenty times, "the SAT is really easy." Before you go to bed, tell yourself, "the SAT is really easy." When you're walking from class to class between periods and have absolutely nothing to do, "the SAT is really easy." When you're on Instagram and your phone tells you how much time you wasted on-screen last week, "the SAT is really easy."

Let me be very clear about this: I'm not telling you the SAT is really easy because it's easy *to me*. I'm telling you it's really easy because it's really easy. I've had middle-school students score 370 and above on the SAT reading exam. Do you know how they were able to do that? Not because they were geniuses by any means. You guessed it! Because the SAT is really easy. The exam is designed for average high-schoolers who have decent critical thinking abilities and can

The SAT is really easy.

interpret information and synthesize coherent and logical arguments. That is a really low bar… because the SAT is really easy.

It matters a lot that you believe me because once you do, it'll save you a ton of time. Certainly, if you've ever taken an SAT, then you've run into one of the following problems:

- you've encountered a word you didn't know
- you've read an entire paragraph and understood absolutely nothing
- you've stared at a question for so long that all the answer choices looked the same
- you've found yourself wavering between two answer choices for a good three minutes before randomly choosing one of the answers and praying you got the question right

Someone who thinks the exam is difficult loses precious time and confidence in all of these situations. But you know the truth: the SAT is really easy. So, when you encounter a word you don't know, it's no problem. You're confident in your vocabulary because you've put in the time and effort to improve your diction. That means that if you see a new or weird word that you can't understand based on context, you know it's probably obscure or irrelevant for interpreting the passage.

When you read a huge chunk of words but totally zone out and have no idea what you just read (we all do it… really, it's okay), you don't get frazzled and start frantically looking at the clock and shaking in your chair because you've wasted some time. You know the test is easy, and you've trained your memory, so you take a deep breath, clear your mind, and dive back in and reread that paragraph like the boss that you are.

And, if you get stuck on a question for more than a minute, you don't fall into a pit of despair and tell yourself you're going to fail and every college is going to reject you. No, no, no. You know way better than to let any question on the SAT have that kind of power over you. Why? Because you're a smart cookie, and if a question on a silly little exam like the SAT is taking up a minute of your time, then there's only one possible explanation: you're overthinking like crazy. Back up, calm down, and strike a yoga pose in your mind (downward dog is always good). Come back to that question a little later when your mind is clearer and you're better able to focus on the simple question the SAT is asking you. Of course, you *will* have time to come back to that question because you're confident and know you'll finish the rest of the questions in a flash. How do I know you will? Because the SAT is really easy.

You'll find by the end of this book that I emphasize confidence a lot. You will not succeed on the SAT without confidence. That's just the simple truth. So, as you continue to read, take special note of my advice regarding confidence. Test anxiety is a legitimate issue that holds far too many students back from achieving their educational goals. The rest of this book focuses on giving you all the tools you need to back up your confidence, but you have to make a promise to yourself that you'll do what it takes to get to that "I'm gonna absolutely destroy this exam because I'm an SAT god" place.

When I ask you to say out loud, "the SAT is really easy," I mean it, and I'm not trying to be funny. Don't say those words to yourself; say them to the universe. When I ask you to keep a running list of new vocabulary words you've encountered, I mean it. I'm not making a suggestion or saying, "Hey, maybe you should try this!" I'm saying you need to do this if you want to learn the words necessary to master the SAT. And when I ask you to read, in print, an article or research paper every day, I mean that you really need to be reading an article or research paper every day if you want to succeed on the exam.

If you take away just one thing from this chapter, I want it to be that you have all the potential to get a perfect score on the SAT reading exam with just a little effort each day. But, if you don't put in the effort, you won't see results. If you don't commit to sharpening your memory, broadening your vocabulary, honing your focus, and boosting your confidence, then you will not improve on the SAT.

Whatever your reason for wanting to improve your score—whether it's to make your parents proud, increase your odds of getting into your dream school, prove your teachers wrong, or just for personal pride—you can do it! Let's realize your dreams and work hard together to make absolute sure you reach your goals.

All right, so where do you go from here? No surprises: it's time to start reading some complex texts! In the next chapter, I show you where to find useful reading materials and break down how you should prepare for each passage type.

CHAPTER THREE

What Do I Read?!

You're ready to start your quest into the world of reading! First things first, though, I need you to have reasonable expectations for yourself. If you're like most other high school students, you've got a huge workload from school, too many extracurriculars to worry about, and manic hormonal fluctuations to deal with. I'm likely not going to be able to convince you to drop social media altogether, and it's not my hope that you'll end up spending four hours each day reading passages to prepare for the SAT. By the way, you should be reading more regardless of the SAT: to be a more informed citizen, to improve your vocabulary, and to improve your critical reading skills. College will be especially difficult for you if you don't develop a habit of reading well and reading often.

My goal is to get you to read for thirty minutes a day—not including the reading you already do (or, at least, are assigned) for classes in school. For two reasons, it is imperative that you read outside of what your teachers assign. First, most of you probably rely on SparkNotes or Shmoop to summarize your readings for you anyways. You read the summaries in preparation for reading quizzes your teachers give you in English class, and you probably never actually read your text. That's okay, and that's your teacher's fault for assigning you reading just for reading's sake. Second, you're almost certainly not at all interested in what your teachers assign you to read. Yes, there is a small group of you saying, "No,

I LOVE Shakespeare," but the rest of us don't. So as to not paint the lily, I'll summarize and move on. You need to read for thirty minutes each day, and assignments for class don't count.

Your response to this task is hopefully, "Great! I'm excited to expand my mind and improve my reading skills! Where do I start?" If that's not your response, say it out loud a few times, and fake it till you make it. Let's start by breaking down the types of passages that you'll encounter on the SAT. I put them into four categories:

1. Straight Up Literature
2. Old People Talking About Politics and Society
3. New People Talking About Politics and Society
4. Summaries of Science Experiments or Studies

The way that you prepare for and approach each passage type is different, so it's of the utmost importance that you understand these differences before you dive headlong into your SAT prep.

1. Straight Up Literature

Straight Up Literature passages, which are always first up on the reading section, are like those that you're used to reading for English class at school. Think, for example, of short stories from Hemingway and Steinbeck or potentially of more recent narrative fiction like *The Hunger Games* or *Twilight*. The pantheon of extant narrative prose is so broad that the SAT can pull passages from the 1800s all the way up to last month, so it's especially important to read from an eclectic mix of genres, subjects, and time periods to adequately prepare yourself for any passage that the SAT throws at you. It's almost impossible that you'll see on the SAT a story you've already read, so your goal isn't to read everything ever written in the hope that you'll be familiar with your reading passages. Instead, your goal should be to familiarize yourself with many different *styles* of prose so that you have unshakeable confidence in your ability to process everything that ends up on the exam.

For whatever reason, this type of passage seems to always be at one extreme or the other for students: it's either dead easy or impossibly difficult. I think that part of the reason for this dichotomy is that many students either read a lot or don't read much at all, with very little in between. Generally, the students who find this section trivially simple are those who read as a consistent pastime.

It's easy to feel down if you don't read much. Don't. A lot of students give up once they feel behind or at a disadvantage. Sure, there are plenty of students who have read a hundred more books than you have. It doesn't matter. All you need to do is to start now. Even if you're a senior, you've never taken an SAT, and it's December, you still have time to boost your reading skill. A little reading each day goes such a long way.

I've put together for you two lists of short stories, essays, and novels that will help you to prepare for your Straight Up Literature passage. The first list contains only texts that are public domain, which means they're available online for free (go to www.gutenberg.org for more free eBooks than you could ever wish for). Remember, you need to read these on paper. I know it's a mild inconvenience. Do it anyways. Print them out or go to your library and check them out—or, ideally, just buy your own used copies of any novels you choose to read from the list. An eReader is not okay for this, and I mean it. I'm not trying to waste your time or money. Research has time and again shown that reading on a screen or any electronic device (even those beautiful Kindle Paperwhites) is far less effective than reading on actual paper.[1]

The second list contains works by more modern authors. Because these authors are more contemporary, their works are generally not public domain, but I am certain you can access online many of their most

---

[1] Check out Nicholas Carr's *What the Internet Is Doing to Our Brains* for a w discussion of this and related topics.

popular publications. You can likely find them in your school or local library. The older works are nearly all by white men, with the exception of those by Charlotte Brontë. This is simply a consequence of the works' being public domain and the historical literary sexism that comes with that age. The newer works run a far more variegated gamut of the race, age, time period, sex, religion, and geographic influences of authors. Because the SAT can throw at you literature from any time period, it's extremely important that you prioritize variety in your reading. Once you feel comfortable with one writer's style, move on to another author.

My hope is that these texts are unfamiliar. Don't reread a text you've already studied closely. You need not read everything from the lists, and if you don't have time to read any novels, then don't read any of the novels. If you do have time but are wasteful and spend most of it on social media or watching Netflix, then cut out some of the junk and read some novels. You'll have plenty of time in the future to watch all the movies, music videos, and makeup tutorials your heart desires, but you've got a very narrow window to prepare for the SAT. Priorities!

None of these works is particularly long, so don't fret. As you go, make sure to write down and memorize any words that are new to you. Remember that short stories are in quotation marks, while novels and anthologies are italicized. The authors are in no particular order.

Classic Works

Arthur Conan Doyle (1859-1930)
    from *The Adventures of Sherlock Holmes**
- "A Scandal in Bohemia"
- "The Five Orange Pips"
- "The Man with the Twisted Lip"
- "The Adventure of the Speckled Band"

- *A Study in Scarlet*
- *The Hound of the Baskervilles*

Jonathan Swift (1667-1745)
- "A Modest Proposal"
- *Gulliver's Travels*

Robert Louis Stevenson (1850-1894)
from *Essays of Travel**
  - "The Sick Man"
  - "New York"
  - "On the Plains"
- *Essays in the Art of Writing**
- *Fables**
- *Strange Case of Dr Jekyll and Mr Hyde*

Charlotte Brontë (1816-1855)
- *Jane Eyre*
- *The Professor*

Charles Dickens (1812-1870)
from *American Notes**
  - "Going Away"
  - "Boston"
  - "Philadelphia, and its Solitary Prison"
- *Dombey and Son*
- *A Tale of Two Cities*

Nathaniel Hawthorne (1804-1864)
from *Twice-Told Tales**
  - "Mr. Higginbotham's Catastrophe"
  - "The Great Carbuncle"
  - "Dr. Heidegger's Experiment"
  - "The Seven Vagabonds"
- *The House of the Seven Gables*

Mark Twain (1835-1910)

- *A Connecticut Yankee in King Arthur's Court*
- *Adventures of Huckleberry Finn*
- "The Celebrated Jumping Frog of Calaveras County"
- "A Dog's Tale"

Edgar Allan Poe (1809-1849)

from *The Works of Edgar Allan Poe, Volume 1**
- "The Murders in the Rue Morgue"
- "The Mystery of Marie Roget"

from *The Works of Edgar Allan Poe, Volume 2**
- "The Purloined Letter"
- "The Pit and the Pendulum"
- "Berenice"

Contemporary Works

Margaret Atwood (1939)

from *Dancing Girls & Other Stories**
- "The Man from Mars"
- "The Resplendent Quetzal"
- *The Handmaid's Tale*
- *Alias Grace*

Alice Walker (1944)

- *The Color Purple*
- *Possessing the Secret of Joy*

Hermann Hesse (1877-1962)

- *Siddhartha*
- *The Glass Bead Game*
- *Journey to the East*

Gary Blackwood (1945)
- *The Shakespeare Stealer*
- *The Year of the Hangman*
- *Around the World in 100 Days*

Ray Bradbury (1920-2012)
- *The Martian Chronicles**
- *Green Shadows, White Whale**
- *Something Wicked This Way Comes*

Harper Lee (1926-2016)
- *To Kill a Mockingbird*
- *Go Set a Watchman*

Amy Tan (1952)
- *The Joy Luck Club*
- *The Bonesetter's Daughter*

Sherman Alexie (1966)
- *Reservation Blues*
- *The Absolutely True Diary of a Part-Time Indian*
- *The Lone Ranger and Tonto Fistfight in Heaven**

Kurt Vonnegut (1922-2007)
from *Welcome to the Monkey House**
  - "Harrison Bergeron"
  - "Tomorrow and Tomorrow and Tomorrow"
  - "Welcome to the Monkey House"
  - "Miss Temptation"
- *Slaughterhouse-Five*

* indicates a collection of poems, essays, or short stories

Again, I don't expect you to get through all of these works any time soon (or ever, for that matter), but I do hope you'll dabble in at least one work or two from each of the authors I've selected. Switch it up as often as possible: read an older short story by a male author one day and a newer chapter from a novel by a female author the next day. The more styles and genres you're familiar with, the better you'll do on the SAT.

At this point, I imagine that you could have two questions. First, *do you really expect me to read* **any** *of these?* and second, *what if I don't like any of these works or authors?* To the first question: Yes, I really do. If you are serious about improving your reading skills, you must read more—there is no exception to this. You can pick up a million different SAT guides and workbooks, but nothing will help you as much as simply reading more. That said, reading alone won't necessarily boost your score—you have to read with the intent to learn (I'll talk about this shortly). Still, if you want a high score on the SAT reading exam, then you need to read more. End of story.

To the second question: Learn to like them. The fact of the matter is that you probably won't be interested in the passages on your actual SAT exam either, so get over it. You may not be interested in the bedraggled love affair between Jane Eyre and Edward Rochester. Maybe it's a little too romantic for your taste. Oh well.[2] You know what you *are* interested in? Getting a perfect score on the SAT and getting tons of scholarship money to whatever college you please. Bite the bullet and jump into some prose you wouldn't ordinarily gravitate toward. You may just find you end up liking romance novels, parodies, and scary stories a lot more than you imagined.

I also want to offer you a bit of reprieve and reassurance: the Straight Up Literature passage is hardest to prepare for, so don't expect

---

2 I wrote this section on the same day I got my flu shot. The nurse warned me that the shot would hurt a little, to which I replied, "better than dying." Apply that mentality to your SAT prep. It hurts a little, and it may be boring, but you want a high score as badly as I want to avoid the flu this year.

long lists of reading suggestions for the other three passage types as well. Also, I don't know about you, but lists scare the heck out of me. I feel insecure if I don't complete everything on a list. Please, please, please do not think you need to read everything here to adequately prepare for the SAT. If you just read a handful (say, two or three of the novels and eight or so of the short stories and essays) of the selections, I'll be thrilled. Read what you can and be reasonable with your expectations.

Now, when you choose to jump into any of these works, what are you actually looking for? For both Straight Up Literature and Old People Talking About Politics and Society passages, be on the lookout for four things: vocabulary, sentence structure, superficial understanding, and deep understanding. Let's together break down a sample passage from Jonathan Swift's "A Modest Proposal":

> *It is a melancholy object to those, who walk through this great town, or travel in the country, when they see the streets, the roads and cabbin-doors crowded with beggars of the female sex, followed by three, four, or six children, all in rags, and importuning every passenger for an alms. These mothers instead of being able to work for their honest livelihood, are forced to employ all their time in stroling to beg sustenance for their helpless infants who, as they grow up, either turn thieves for want of work, or leave their dear native country, to fight for the Pretender in Spain, or sell themselves to the Barbadoes.*

Let's consider first the vocabulary. You must be judicious when deciding what to add to your running list of new words. Don't include what's unimportant: alternative spellings, irrelevant references, and rare-but-easy words. Here, for example, "cabbin" is simply an alternative spelling of "cabin," as is "stroling" an alternative to "strolling." Furthermore, "the Pretender in Spain" refers to the son of King James

II, who was deposed in 1688. That's useless information in context; the SAT isn't a history exam, and you should be confident that any relevant historical or literary references or allusions will be explained in the footnotes of your SAT passage. Lastly, don't waste your time on rare-but-easy words like "employ" as it is used in this excerpt. Rarely, if ever, would I talk about how I employ my time because I'm not that important. I definitely use, waste, and even allot my time, but I never employ it. Nevertheless, I still understand what Swift means when he says that mothers "employ [use] all their time" with their children, and this word stays off my vocab list. As a general rule of thumb, if you understand precisely what a word means in context, even if the phrasing is a little unusual, then don't bother with it, and revel in your ability to adapt.

What absolutely *does* belong on your vocab list are—and this should at this point be old news to you—completely new words and words used in ways unfamiliar to you. I am near certain you don't, or didn't until a minute ago, know what the word "importune" means.[3] On the list it goes, with some clever ways to remember it. Perhaps "melancholy" and "sustenance" and "alms" are also unfamiliar to you, so throw those on the list as well. Moreover, the word "want" is used in a somewhat unfamiliar way here—at least if you don't know all the definitions for the word. You obviously know what I mean if I say I want a slice of pizza, but would someone turn into a thief because he or she wanted work? I mean, maybe? But if you know that "want," when used as a noun, means lack or dearth, then "turn thieves for want of work" suddenly makes a whole lot more sense. This, too, goes on your list! Once you've figured out what these words mean, go back, reread the passage, and see if it makes a bit more sense to you. It invariably will.

Next, you'll want to familiarize yourself with any awkward, stylistic, or confusing sentence structures you find in your readings.

---

3 It means to harass or beg someone for something, especially in the case of seeking a courtesan (look that one up, but not on Google Images).

Crucially, especially in the case of older texts, do not seek to emulate the punctuation and convoluted sentence structures these authors use. These authors abuse commas and incomplete sentences left and right, since grammar and punctuation rules have only recently become standardized. I'm not asking you to start writing like Jonathan Swift or Edgar Allan Poe; I'm asking you to get used to their complex sentences so that you're not flustered when you see similar writing styles on the SAT.

With few exceptions, we're generally used to speaking, writing, and reading English in subject-verb-object (SVO) syntax:

I (subject) want (verb) a cookie (object).

My mom and I (subject) ultimately decided (verb) that we'd donate our books to charity (object).[4]

Donald Trump (subject) was elected (verb) president (object).

This is the order of words we're accustomed to, so we get a little scared when we see alterations to or complications of this general recipe, and that's okay. The more you read, the less these alternative syntaxes will bother you. Consider the sentence "Absent from all his lectures was any consideration for communicative ease." It sounds a little janky and old-fashioned, doesn't it? What I basically mean is "His lectures were hard to understand," but because I've rearranged the sentence structure (the original is VSO), I've made it just a bit tougher to comprehend. These sentences aren't particularly complicated, just unfamiliar.

Other times, authors may follow SVO structure but just craft downright complicated sentences. Swift, for example, opens "A Modest Proposal" with a Brobdingnagian sentence: "It is a melancholy object to

---

4 For the grammarians among you, rest easy that I know it's a bit simplistic to call this just an "object," but that's more or less its function in the sentence.

those, who walk through this great town, or travel in the country, when they see the streets, the roads and cabbin-doors crowded with beggars of the female sex, followed by three, four, or six children, all in rags, and importuning every passenger for an alms." When we read a lengthy sentence like this, our first instinct is to tilt our heads back, roll our eyes, and sigh. That's totally acceptable. After you've let out your literary ire, compose yourself and try to piece the sentence together. Can we distill it down to a simpler sentence that isn't nearly as sinuous? Yes! Read in chunks, figure out what you know, and construct meaning little-by-little.

Here's what the sentence is essentially saying: It sucks when you see women and children begging in the streets. Can you translate from the original to my simplified version? This is effectively making sense of the superficial meaning—or, as some would disdainfully say, the plot—of a text. As you're reading, perform this type of distillation, and then reread the original sentences to demystify their complexity. If you like to annotate, this is a good place to focus your annotations. As you read, briefly reflect on confusing passages and write your simplified versions in the margins. This makes it easier to review the sequence of events in a passage once you've finished reading, which will save you a lot of skimming time when you get around to the questions.

> *No one is born reading Shakespeare.*

I promise you that the more you read, the more naturally translating what seems like esoterica will come to you. Give yourself the time to gather that experience, and the results will follow. Perhaps you have friends who are "better readers" than you; they're just more experienced. No one is born reading Shakespeare.

Finally, let's attack the issue of deeper meaning in these passages. English teachers have ingrained in us something of a psychosis: how many times have you heard an English teacher say, "but what does the author *really* mean?" Certainly, very many times authors write with incredibly rich subtext that far transcends the literal meaning of their narratives. But reader beware. Not everything has a deeper meaning.

Alas, we're taught the precise opposite since at least kindergarten. Why, for instance, is the American flag red, white, and blue? "The red represents courage," our teachers assuredly proclaimed, "the white stands for purity, and the blue means justice." But, like, do they, though? Did anyone ever consider the possibility that those colors just kinda… look nice together? Or that maybe red and blue dye were cheapest at the time? Or maybe that's just the fabric Betsy Ross (who, by the way, didn't even design the flag—sorry to crush your dreams) had on-hand? An author writing a novel has hundreds of pages to fill; do you think every word is a big deal to write? Yeah, maybe on page 284 of a novel some room is white, but does that really matter? Probably not.[5]

That said, deeper meaning is out there, and you have to be able to decipher it. Rest assured that the SAT isn't going to pull a passage from James Joyce and ask you to analyze the meaning of life. The SAT will, however, expect you to make sense of mood and character relationships as revealed through sensory details.

So far as mood is concerned, pay acutely close attention to the environment in a text and ask yourself whether its state or change of state reflects that of a character or situation. Or, simply, does the setting mirror the characters? If the author bothers to tell you that, while two characters are talking, the clouds overhead suddenly turn dark and block the sun, then that probably means the story is heading in a (literally) dark direction. Is there reason for any character to be sad, depressed, or dejected? Has the author just revealed a betrayal? Does the shift in scenery mark a transition in the way a character acts or speaks for the remainder of the narrative? Make note (annotations) of these details because the SAT absolutely loves to ask about them.

---

5 On the contrary, in a short story nearly every detail has significance.

Regarding character relationships, by the end of a passage, you should reliably be able to construct a "tonal family tree" of the characters. What I mean by this is that you should be able to map both simple relationships (Is character A the brother, sister, boss, nephew, or husband of character B?) and complex relationships (How does character A *feel* about character B? Has their relationship changed over time?).

Authors usually don't obscure the simple relationships, so if you find yourself at a complete loss for understanding the simple relationship between two or more characters, then perhaps the author never reveals it (or, as in *The Empire Strikes Back*, perhaps the reveal is actually the climax of the story). You're looking for keywords like "brother" here to tell you that two characters are brothers. It's not rocket science, so don't make it tough on yourself. If a passage says, "Juan and Carlito are brothers," and then one of the questions asks you how Juan and Carlito are related, don't sit there thinking that there's gotta be something more to the question. They're brothers. The SAT is really easy, remember?

Tougher are the questions that focus on tonal relationships, especially when vocab gets in the way. How do the characters talk to each other? What happens to the surroundings when those characters interact? Do you know anything about the characters' body language? Here's a short excerpt from a story I wrote a few years ago:

> *His vituperative howls scythed my gut. My blood*
> *congealed. My face blanched. I watched as my life played*
> *in an adrenaline-accelerated reverse.*

If you don't know what vituperative, scythe, congeal, or blanch means, then you're probably at a complete loss for the mood here. Notice I said "or" because if you know even one of those words, then you unlock most of the meaning. Otherwise, consider the possible situations. Am I at a concert? Am I hunting a wolf? Am I in a job interview? Is my dad scolding me? Learn your vocab.

If I had instead said, "His mean yelling cut my stomach. My blood froze. My face turned completely white. My life flashed before my eyes," you might have had a far better shot at ascertaining something nearer to the actual context, which was that some drunk guy in a parking lot pulled a gun on me because he thought I was trying to steal his car. Your ability to understand character interactions depends on your vocab.

So, when an author tells you that a character "yelled" or "screeched" or "erupted" at another character, take note. The SAT frequently asks about these types of relationships in "what's your evidence" form: those questions that go, "Which of the following choices provides the best evidence for your answer to the previous question?"

If you are very serious about attuning yourself to the deeper meaning of texts beyond just character-character interactions and mood, then you definitely need to read Thomas C. Foster's *How to Read Literature Like a Professor*. He'll guide you through the nuance and "hidden meaning" of pretty much every possible literary scenario. Some of what he outlines is outside the scope of the SAT, but much of his insight is extremely helpful.

Many students are confused about what it means to be able to analyze a text. They think that analyzing means writing a five-page essay about symbolism. So, I know that some of you are out there thinking *I bought this book expecting this guy would teach me how to analyze, but all he told me was that I have to learn vocab, have confidence, and read more!* The notion that you need to recognize every allusion and symbol in a text in order to appreciate its meaning is a total lie. What matters more than anything else is whether you can understand a story at the plot level.

The question "How do I improve my critical thinking?" is really "How do I understand what's going on?" What presently holds you back from making sense of stories? If you're like most students, then your primary barriers to understanding narratives are your focus, your vocabulary, and your familiarity with writing styles. If you can't focus on a story, then you can't follow its plot. Losing focus while reading is like going to the bathroom during a movie: if you're not there, you don't know what's going on. And when your vocabulary is weak, you miss meaning as well. Just because it's English doesn't mean it can't be foreign to you. Finally, if you've flat out never read a novel in your life, then you can't possibly expect yourself to be familiar with the patterns and writing styles that you'll encounter in fiction. What I've taught you *is* analysis.

To aid you in your quest toward understanding literary narratives, I have provided you with a worksheet to accompany any short story or chapter that you read. You can access this worksheet any time at www.tutorjacob.com/s/straightupliterature.pdf. For your convenience, I have also provided in the Appendix a copy of this worksheet and the worksheets for the other passage types. It's not so important that you actually fill out the worksheet as that you consider the questions every time you read. Now, go forth into the world of narrative fiction!

2. Old People Talking About Politics and Society

If you've just read the "Straight Up Literature" section of this chapter, then you already know much of what you need for this second type of passage: Old People Talking About Politics and Society—or, even more pointedly, old white people and Frederick Douglass talking about the world. To destroy this section, you need a strong vocabulary (surprised?) and a basic knowledge of American history. That's all.

As you might imagine, the vocabulary in these passages is different from the vocabulary in Straight Up Literature passages. A writer arguing for women's suffrage is going to draw from a different set of words than would someone like Nathaniel Hawthorne drafting *The House of the Seven Gables*. Therefore, you should prepare for these passages separately, and it may help you to even keep a separate vocabulary list for these texts.

So far as history knowledge is concerned, my assumption is that anyone reading this book knows who George Washington, Thomas Jefferson, Frederick Douglass, and Abraham Lincoln are. If, by chance, you happen to not know who any of these men are, then you should spend a little time on Crash Course American History on YouTube to familiarize yourself with the basics of US history and politics. Even if you know the big names, you're probably not as familiar with such figures as Mary Wollstonecraft, Edmund Burke, Ida B. Wells, and Booker T. Washington, among others. These writers come up often on the SAT, so it's tremendously helpful if you understand where they fit in a historical and political context. Please commit the following few details to memory:

Mary Wollstonecraft (1759-1797)
- English writer and champion of women's rights
- wrote *A Vindication of the Rights of Woman*
- argued that women and men should be equals, especially regarding access to education

Elizabeth Cady Stanton (1815-1902)
- American writer and champion of women's rights
- along with Lucretia Mott and others, organized the Seneca Falls Convention, a conference for women's rights
- wrote the Declaration of Rights and Sentiments, a pastiche of the Declaration of Independence, which argues that men had unfairly oppressed women in American society, just as King George III had unfairly oppressed the colonists

Edmund Burke (1729-1797)
- Irish writer and politician who was a member of the British House of Commons (the British equivalent of our House of Representatives)
- implored British Parliament to peacefully negotiate with the American colonists
- respected the monarchy of Britain but also recognized how unfairly Britain treated the American colonists

Ida B. Wells (1862-1931)

- African-American journalist and activist
- born a slave and freed by the Emancipation Proclamation
- argued and fought for racial equality: she was one of the founders of the NAACP

W.E.B. Du Bois (1868-1963)

- African-American academic and activist
- not born a slave and was highly educated in the American university system (he was the first African American to earn a PhD from Harvard)
- fought for swift and total integration of Blacks into American society

Booker T. Washington (c. 1856-1915)

- African-American author and activist
- born a slave and freed by the Emancipation Proclamation
- argued and fought for racial equality, but was more willing to compromise than Ida B. Wells or W.E.B. Du Bois
- strong proponent of educating Black Americans as a method to decrease their (forced) reliance on whites

Henry David Thoreau (1817-1862)

- American transcendentalist philosopher and writer
- wrote *Walden*, which extols the value of connecting with nature, and "Civil Disobedience," which criticizes the flaws in American government
- was a strong abolitionist, and his works influenced Gandhi, Martin Luther King, and many other civil activists who came after him

Familiarity with these names will curb potential anxiety: *Who is that? Oh my god I have no idea what's going on here! I'll never get into college!* You'll feel comforted to encounter a writer whose name you're familiar with. *Oh that guy!* Instead of getting lost in the historical fray, you'll be grounded in cozy and relatable territory—and you'll then free up all your attention to focus on the actual content of the passage (you know, the stuff you need for answering the questions).

You need to read Old People Talking About Politics and Society passages as often as possible. Any text that will help you prepare for this passage will be available free online. Many others have already compiled what I think are strong, comprehensive lists of such texts. Ivy Global, at www.sat.ivyglobal.com/great-global-conversation, has a great list of founding American documents and famous Western political speeches. For other resources, just type in "SAT Great Global Conversation" to Google, and you'll find all manner of texts to prepare for this passage.

What you'll initially find most difficult about these passages is that their vocabulary and sentence structures are dated—they'll definitely feel old to you (if they don't, find different passages to read). Luckily, there are many resources—SparkNotes, Shmoop, and CliffsNotes—that have posted great analyses and summaries of these older texts. So, while you might initially get lost in the quagmire of yore, the internet will help you out, in just the same way that *No Fear Shakespeare* demystifies Shakespeare's often indecipherable prose. Your goal is to develop familiarity (did I mention that familiarity is key?) with older texts to the point that they don't sound old to you anymore.

My English teacher in freshman year of high school would often wax romantic about how she "just got" Shakespeare, meaning that, for whatever reason,[6] Shakespeare just sounded like normal English to her, and there was no need to translate it to modern Standard American English. What she really meant was that she had, through repeat exposure and

---

6 The reason was that she had taught British Literature for decades...

trial and error, learned the dialect of Shakespearean English. If you know multiple languages, then you understand very well that the more you read, speak, and write in another language, the greater your facility with that language. Ergo, the more you read, speak, and write like the public figures of days past, the better you'll be able to understand Old People Talking About Politics and Society passages. It's not brain surgery, and it can be really fun! Just ask Lin-Manuel Miranda, who wrote *Hamilton*.

As you read through these old passages, make note of the unfamiliar: sentence structure, syntax (e.g., do these authors tend to place adverbs in weird places in their sentences?), and especially vocabulary. Importantly, a lot of the political vocabulary of the old days carries over to today. We do, not shockingly, inherit much of our political lexicon from British and Colonial-American political parlance. As always, keep a running list of these new encounters, and make every effort possible to incorporate them into your own vocabulary and writing style. There is no greater source of high school intellectual pride than learning a complex word and then seeing it used somewhere else. *Yeah, I know what that word means. Doesn't everyone?! You mean you don't read the Federalist Papers for leisure?! Heathen.* Embrace your inner literary genius.

I provide you with a worksheet for this passage type as well, which is available at www.tutorjacob.com/s/oldsociety.pdf and in the Appendix. Again, prioritize understanding above all else. If you can recognize what these authors (and speakers, as many of these works are speeches) are saying on the surface, then you're ready for the SAT. In effect, all you have to do is learn to translate these texts to modern English. The more you do this, the easier it will become.

3. New People Talking About Politics and Society

The obvious difference between this type of passage and the previous type is that New People Talking About Politics and Society passages are—you guessed it!—newer. What this means is that you get a break from the vocabulary and syntactical circus that older writers employed. Hooray! These newer passages place a far greater emphasis on incorporating data and statistics to prove sociological or political theses. For these passages, you need to focus much more on the logic behind authors' conclusions by answering the following questions:

- What historical trend or problem led this author to conduct his/her research?
- What predictions or preconceptions (assumptions) does the author make?
- What are the actual data the author collected, and where are the data from? How were they obtained?
- How does the author interpret these data? Do the data support the author's claims?
- In what ways does the author suggest that his/her conclusions warrant further research?
- Why is this research important? Why should the author's conclusions matter to us?

Luckily for you, authors tend to answer these questions in this order because it makes the most structural sense. In any New People Talking About Politics and Society passage you read, you need to answer these questions, so I've packaged them and a few other questions in a worksheet, available at www.tutorjacob.com/s/newsociety.pdf as well as the Appendix. Answer these questions every time you read one of these passages, without exception. Your goal should never be to read just for the sake of reading. Read because you want to learn something new, explore new potential interests, and expand your outlook on the world. Read because you want to increase your fluency in English and your ability to communicate complex ideas with others. In the simplest terms, if you don't understand what you're reading, then you're not actually reading... you're just looking at words to pass the time.

Any of these well-edited publications will be rife with articles that fall into this category:

- *The New York Times*
- *The Atlantic*
- *The Wall Street Journal*
- *The Economist*
- *The New Yorker*
- *Time*

I'm partial to *The New Yorker*, but any of these will do. Make an effort to read these sources in print. Even for such reputable sources as these, I can't tell you how many times I've encountered severe online typographical errors that we want to avoid at all costs. Just because their magazines are typo-free doesn't mean that their websites are. These publications invest far more editorial resources into their print copy than their web copy. There won't be typos on the SAT, so why should you read practice texts with typos? Feel free to read any article on any subject in these publications, and vary your focus as often as possible: read an economics article one day and a literature review the next day.

Reddit is also a tremendous source for these passages. Venture over to www.reddit.com/r/science, and you can narrow the articles down to social science articles (click the "Social" button in the header menu) and from there narrow to either anthropology, economics, psychology, or social science. Sort by "top" if you want to view the most popular submitted articles from the past day, week, month, or even all time. You can also find great articles on the Economics, WorldNews, and Politics subreddits. The URL for any subreddit is www.reddit.com/r/sub_name.

When reading these passages, as always take note of any unfamiliar vocabulary or new ideas, and otherwise all you need to do is answer the questions I gave you. What's especially great about finding articles through Reddit is that you can then pore over the wealth of questions and comments that users have submitted about those articles. If you don't understand something, it's likely someone else doesn't either, so scroll through the comments and find answers to your questions. Flex your academic exploratory muscle (your brain) and get going on fostering your fluency with New People Talking About Politics and Society passages. A whole new world of experiments, ideas, and wacky truths about human behavior awaits you!

4. Summaries of Science Experiments or Studies

We're in the home stretch! Propitiously for us, the science passages are the most predictable and redundant (read as: easiest to prepare for) of all the passages on the SAT Reading. Every passage follows the same rough outline:

- Background
- Hypothesis
- Procedure
- Results
- Significance

You'll notice this is similar to the general structure of New People Talking About Politics and Society passages: social science is science, after all. What I've found very troubling for students is that they simply don't recognize that science passages follow this outline. So, when students come across a line like, "Then Dr. Hiller and her team split the group into halves, with the first half receiving the extra calcium supplement and the second half receiving a placebo," even though this is textbook procedure/method, they can't see the function of the information in the context of the passage (it's just procedure).

Every science passage you read will follow this outline, so get to recognizing the structure of this pattern. Again, so important is practicing this that I've created a science passage worksheet, which is in the Appendix and available at www.tutorjacob.com/s/science.pdf. Have this with you whenever you're reading a science passage.

Finding science articles is super easy. Again navigate over to reddit.com/r/science, but this time filter the posts by life or physical science. You can also find science articles in the following publications:

- *National Geographic*
- *Popular Mechanics*
- *Scientific American*
- *Smithsonian*
- *Popular Science*
- *Discover*

What's more difficult is determining whether any given science article is worth reading. Here are a couple of guidelines to follow when deciding on a passage to read for science practice:

- If the article has photos, that's a good sign. You mostly want to read articles that are secondary sources, and writers of secondary sources usually include photos in their articles.
- Better yet, if an article contains graphs, tables, or other figures that display data from a study, that's a great sign.
- If you find an article that isn't free, then don't bother.
- Articles from scientific journals are beyond the scope of SAT science passages. If you see headers like "Abstract," "Methodology," and "Results," odds are you're looking at a journal article. Find something else instead.
- Proper science articles for your SAT practice should be about one to two pages long. You've seen the articles on actual SATs— they should be of that length.

Some science passages are too complex or written in a style totally distinct from the style of the passages you'll see on the SAT. Primary sources (actual studies themselves, as opposed to reports *about* those studies) usually fall into this category. Reading them will help you prepare for college-level science classes but not for the SAT. Once you've found a good article, print it out, read it through, and complete the corresponding worksheet. In just a few weeks, you'll find that your ability to read and understand scientific texts is extraordinary. You will literally laugh at how easy these passages are to comprehend.

Read with purpose and target specific skills whenever you delve into a new passage. Use the worksheets I've given you as a guide for this. If you run into questions that you can't answer, then use the internet to your advantage. If you encounter quotes or italics or evidence or data or phrases or concessions or arguments that you can't understand in context, then ask a forum or post your question on Reddit. There are so many people out there willing to help you and answer your questions, but you have to ask them first!

After about a month of solid reading practice (read *at least* one article a day, and vary passage types as often as possible), you should then start to occasionally incorporate practice exams into your prep routine. Again, first put in the effort to building your reading fluency, and only thereafter start weaving practice tests in. Practice tests are completely useless if you haven't first built your skills as a reader. You can't run a marathon without some training first! Once you're ready, venture into Chapter Four to learn everything you need to know about taking practice exams.

CHAPTER FOUR

Practice Tests

Now that you're a veteran reader who's starting to develop a strong vocabulary, you're ready to venture into the world of practice exams. I cannot possibly overemphasize that practice exams are assessment tools first and learning tools a not-at-all-close second. One of the biggest mistakes that students make is to squander all the available practice exams before learning their fundamentals. If you have not already read the previous chapters, then you need to go and read them before proceeding (unless you're taking the exam very, very soon and lack the time to properly prepare).

I've already told you that another terrible mistake students make is to use practice exams that aren't official. Using unofficial practice exams is an absolute waste of your time. Don't do it. I say that not because I think the College Board is necessarily better than Kaplan or other practice test providers. In fact, I prefer the types of questions that some prep books ask to the types of questions that the real SAT asks—but that doesn't matter because the College Board writes the real SAT, and you don't send your Kaplan diagnostic scores to any universities.

Have you ever used a different keyboard and found it, at least initially, very difficult to type on, even though you've had years of typing experience? A new keyboard is *close*, but it's not *exactly* what you're used to. Maybe you've broken school records swimming freestyle. Does that make you the best at backstroke? Perhaps you've mastered an etude on your piano keyboard, which lacks weighted keys. Try to play that etude on a Steinway, and it's a whole different ballgame. If you want perfection, then *close* just doesn't cut it.

The point is this: the SAT test writers design the official exam with consistency in mind, but the nuances of SAT reading questions never completely carry over to unofficial practice exams. Even if a practice exam is 95% similar to the real SAT, why not take an exam that actually is a 100% real SAT? Repeat after me: *I shall not take unofficial practice exams.* As of my writing this text, there are at least sixteen[1] released official SAT practice tests. Simply search Google for "SAT QAS Reddit" to find a list of these documents. And though there are sure to be more practice tests available in the near future, if you approach your practice exams correctly, you won't need anywhere near even these sixteen.

On the College Board's website,[2] you can find eight full-length official practice SATs, complete with answer keys, scoring guidelines, and answer explanations. Start with these exams first, since their answer explanations will prove very helpful in your prep: they tell you exactly what reading skills the SAT test-writers value. You shouldn't need to use all eight of these to get yourself to perfect-score level, but if you exhaust all the official practice exams, then move to the eight released QAS (Question & Answer Service) packages, which many students have posted on Reddit and other websites. The QAS exams do not come with answer explanations, but they are still official College Board SATs. In fact, these exams are SATs that have recently been used as official SATs.

Using anywhere near all the available exams is a huge red flag and indicates a poor SAT prep regimen. You cannot rely on practice tests.

---

1 Many international students have illicitly obtained copies of unreleased exams, and an April 2019 QAS might soon become available, so this number is doubtless lower than the true number of exams out in the wild.

2 http://www.collegereadiness.collegeboard.org/sat/practice/full-length-practice-tests

Why do you take practice SAT exams? Have you ever really considered this? Perhaps the answer seems obvious to you: *Duh! For practice!* But what does that actually mean? What are you actually practicing when you take a practice test? Just like you need to read with purpose, you need to take practice tests with purpose. Don't follow your teachers' model here; don't take practice tests just 'cause. Your approach to the SAT or any academic pursuit should have structure and intent.

Let's say you've never heard or read a lick of Spanish in your life, and I ask you to translate the following sentence: *Después del juego, todos fuimos a la tienda a comprar un nuevo cepillo de dientes para el perro del vecino.* Would you have the slightest clue in the world what that means? What if I asked you to translate fifteen other sentences—would that teach you anything? Would you get better at translating Spanish to English if I never taught you Spanish vocabulary or grammar? Of course not. Exams are not learning tools. If you don't have the skills to begin with, then it's impossible to practice those skills.

You don't learn to become a better critical reader simply by taking more practice SATs. (For that matter, you don't learn math concepts or grammar rules by taking more practice SATs, either.) You don't learn new words simply by taking more practice SATs. The majority of your preparation for the SAT should come outside of practice exams. They are there to familiarize you with the structure and format of the SAT and to help you keep track of your progress over time. Specifically, they reveal to you what areas you can still improve in and what types of questions you struggle with. But once you use an exam to identify weaknesses to target, you shouldn't go and take another exam right after. You have to go and work on those weaknesses! Find new reading materials and focus on developing the skills that you lacked during your last practice exam.

Before we go on, here are a few ground rules:

1. Official SATs only! (Official PSATs are okay too.)
2. Make sure you tabulate your score with the correct scale (e.g., don't score Practice Test 8 with the scale from Practice Test 2).
3. Always print out practice exams. Just as your real test will be on paper, so too should your practice tests be on paper.
4. Mimic testing conditions as best you can. If you plan to wear a watch on test day, then wear a watch during your practice exam. The same goes for pajamas, hats, slippers, etc. Even use the same pencil and eraser. If you can, take practice exams on Saturday mornings, just like the real exam.
5. To get your mind into critical reading mode, read a short story, an article, or a chapter from one of your favorite novels before you take any SAT.
6. Take the entire reading section in one sitting. Don't start by practicing individual passages. If you're practicing for other sections as well, then take the entire exam in one sitting.
7. Get pumped. Have I mentioned that confidence is important? Before you take any test, play the most upbeat, motivating, energizing song you know. Stretch out your arms. Let out a howl if need be. You're literally an animal, so let the blood flow.
8. Limit your exposure to the color pink. I love pink, but research shows that pink hues legitimately make you weaker. Seriously. Google "Baker-Miller pink."
9. Time yourself. That doesn't necessarily mean you have to stop once time runs out; it just means you need to keep track of how much time you spend on each practice test.
10. Don't take the same practice test twice. If this conflicts with rule number one, then—and it pains me to say this—use an unofficial practice test… but only if there really isn't a single official practice test that you haven't already taken!

Now you're ready to start your practice test journey. If you've bought this book, you've probably taken at least a practice exam or two, and you're likely already familiar with the format and types of questions on the SAT reading exam. If you've never taken an official SAT practice test, then the main purpose of your first one should be to accustom yourself to the layout and structure of the exam. Don't put an anvil on your shoulders and stress out about your score or whether you're finishing on-time or whether you'll ever get into college. Just get used to the

A good idea is to actually read the questions aloud.

exam. On past multiple-choice exams, you've likely not seen questions of the form "Which of the following provides the best evidence for the answer to the previous question?" The SAT is unique. Simply digest the types of questions the SAT asks you. If any question seems difficult, remind yourself that you must be overthinking. The SAT is an easy exam, remember? Time yourself but go overtime if needed.

A good idea for your first practice exam is to actually read the questions aloud, which gives you a sense of proper pacing and the way the SAT phrases its questions. I couldn't tell you how many times I've just read a question out loud to a student only to hear that tired response, "Oh *that's* what they were asking!" Don't neglect to answer the questions they actually ask, which starts with carefully reading those questions.

During the test, **mark any questions you're unsure about**. Yes, I bolded *and* italicized that dollop of advice. Don't just review the questions you get wrong. Mark any answers you're even one percent unsure of and review those questions just the same as you would review the questions you miss. Just because you get a question right on one exam doesn't mean you'll get a similar question right on another exam. This goes back to the distinction between being *good* and being *great*. I want you to be great, which means you should know how to properly answer *every* question on the SAT reading exam. A 25% chance (randomly guessing correctly) or a 50% chance (narrowing down to two answers and luckily choosing the right one) is not the mark of a great test-taker. You're better than that, so practice all your weak points, correct or not.

After you finish your exam, go and take a break—say, a half-hour or so. Give that high-vocabulary, critical-thinking brain some rest. There's no rush, and a nice stretch, glass of water, and maybe even a quick meditation session will allow you to stay focused and energized when you decide to come back to assess your results. How you diagnose your performance—that is, whether you can accurately and reliably identify areas for improvement—will determine whether you get a perfect score and save time by only reading passages that address your vulnerabilities... or get a mediocre score and waste time by reading passages that don't improve your reading skills. So, you need to go into this process refreshed, optimistic, and punctilious. Ultimately, this is the gatekeeper to SAT reading prowess. Take it seriously and read over the remainder of this chapter at least twice before catapulting yourself backward into the land of "I thought I was better" and "I'll never break 350."

I want to digress for just a moment and remind you that it's okay to feel down at times. Over the years, I've never met a student who was always optimistic, always happy, or always right. We all make mistakes, we all flunk exams, and we all get down on ourselves when we think we've failed. We've all felt like the world is conspiring against us and that, no matter how hard we try or how much we study or exercise or practice, we'll never be good enough for our parents, for our loved ones, or for ourselves. There is not a soul alive or dead who never felt like this.

What separates those of us who ultimately succeed from those of us who stay forever consigned to a station of pity, pessimism, and poverty (be it spiritual, academic, or monetary) are our outlooks. You've heard it repeated by the truckload, "It's not about how many times you get knocked down but how many times you get back up." That is terrible advice. It's not true, and it overlooks the critical importance of strategy, creativity, flexibility, and adaptation. Hard work isn't always good.

I played tackle football in middle school, and one day at practice my teammate knocked me down so hard that I broke my ankle. I got back up… and I quit. My parents were furious: "We didn't raise a quitter," they told me. In fact, my dad initially refused to take me to the doctor and insisted I just needed to "walk it off." I felt ashamed. Didn't hard work mean braving the pain and going back to playing football?

Absolutely not! If some process, activity, strategy, or person causes you to fail miserably, then unless you want more failure, get that thing out of your life. Einstein likely never said it, but it's sage advice no less: doing the same thing over and over and expecting a different outcome is insane.[3] To this day, quitting football is probably the best decision I ever made. Yeah, I got back up—what, was I gonna stay on the ground, writhing in pain forever?—but I sure didn't play football ever again.

So, should you find that your practice test score is astronomically lower than you'd hoped, the constructive response is absolutely *not* to tell yourself, "Well, I'll try again next time and hope I improve! I won't give up!" There's no pride in "not giving up." Simply doubling down on the same mistaken strategy doesn't make you resilient; it makes you stubborn. If you find yourself knocked down by your SAT reading

> *Get back up and then change something.*

score, then you've really been knocked down by your lack of reading strategy, vocabulary, and focus. Get back up and then change something.

---

3 First Betsy Ross… and now Einstein?!

Now that you're rejuvenated and you've graded your exam,[4] it's time you approach what I call The Big Three—the three questions you need to ask and answer for every single question you missed or didn't understand:

1. Why are the three wrong answers absolutely, positively, not kinda-sorta but downright, totally, beyond-the-shadow-of-a-doubt incorrect?
2. Why is the right answer certainly, legitimately, make-no-mistake-about-it, definitely, cross-your-heart-and-hope-to-die correct?
3. What could you have done differently—and, infinitely more importantly, what will you do differently next time—that would have allowed you to answer the question correctly?

Answer these questions for every single problem you have. If, on your first practice exam, you miss 13 questions and are unsure about an additional 4 (these categories are not mutually exclusive), then you've got 17 rounds of The Big Three ahead of you. At first, it may seem cumbersome to do this for so many questions. You'll inevitably find yourself making excuses: "Oh, I see what I did, just a silly mistake. I don't need The Big Three for this question." *No!* If you missed or struggled with a question, break out The Big Three—no exceptions and

> *Do you want a perfect score? Don't cut corners.*

---

4 Please grade carefully! Download the Daily Practice for the SAT app, which will automatically grade and scale your official practice tests.

no excuses. Do you want a perfect score? Don't cut corners. On the reading exam, there's no such thing as a silly mistake. As you improve (and you'll improve quickly, I guarantee it), you'll have fewer Big-Three rounds, so don't fret.

1. Why are the wrong answers wrong?

One of the scariest horror stories I know goes like this: One of the students in an SAT class asks his teacher why #31 on the reading section is B instead of A. "Choice A," the student reasons, "seems to be supported by the sentence that begins at line 84. I see that B also has textual support because the last sentence of the passage is basically a restatement of choice B, but what makes A wrong?" The teacher, after skimming back through the passage and mulling over the student's question, responds, "You're right. A and B are both supported by the passage, and it's really tough to decide between the two choices, so you just have to go for the one that sounds better."

I know! It sends shivers down *my* spine, too, every time I hear it! This really may be the worst advice for the SAT reading exam—and it's advice that I've woefully seen proclaimed by some prep books, YouTube videos, and even one of my old colleagues in his SAT class. "Go for the one that sounds better"? What does that even mean??? If you ever have an SAT tutor or teacher who brings this horror story to life, Marie Kondo 'em into the trash. Fast. That does *not* spark joy. (This terrible "advice" is almost as unforgivably erroneous and deleterious as "So long as you work hard, you'll be fine." More on that one a little later.) Accept this as dogma: There is no such thing as a good wrong answer.

For every question on the SAT reading exam, there are three wrong answers, and they're all unapologetically wrong. Really, the whole SAT boils down to categorizing answers. Your task is to figure out what kind of wrong answers you're dealing with, leaving the correct one behind. Once you can identify that an answer is incorrect, answering a question becomes that much easier. I highly recommend using process of elimination and looking at every answer choice for every question. Sometimes, an answer choice looks good at first but emerges as clearly incorrect on a second inspection. If you look at an answer and immediately jump to bubble it in before you consider all the answer choices, you're doing yourself a disservice. Be patient and thorough. Simply enough, all answers come in one of just four flavors:

- False
- True but irrelevant
- True but not supported by the passage
- True and the correct answer

The faster you can start throwing answers into these categories (and all answers fall into one of these four), the faster you'll start improving your SAT reading score.[5]

False Wrong Answers

False Case 1: The passage explicitly states the opposite of what an answer choice says. This is an obvious one, but these answers are sometimes hard to identify if your vocabulary is lacking. If a passage says, "The painting was sundered by the earthquake," and an answer choice says, "The painting miraculously survived the earthquake intact," then the answer choice would be incorrect, since to sunder is to split apart. Remember when I said vocabulary was, like, super-duper important? If you can find textual evidence that disproves an answer choice, then physically cross that answer choice out. It's wrong.

---

5 Don't assume that because there are four categories and four answers for each question that each answer choice has to uniquely correspond to one of these categories. You could, for example, run into a question for which all three wrong answers are false.

False Case 2: The passage says something similar to what an answer choice says, but the answer choice inappropriately and without evidence generalizes to an extreme or extrapolates (draws another related conclusion from the same premise) to another unsubstantiated specific. For example, if a passage tells you that Jonathan has a young son who cried himself to sleep last night, you may see answer choices that say, "Jonathan's young son always cries himself to sleep," (a false generalization—we don't know that he *always* cries himself to sleep) or, "Jonathan was angry with his son for crying so much last night" (an unsubstantiated extrapolation—even though many parents bemoan their children's whining, unless the passage states it, we can't be sure that our Jonathan was angry with his son). A variation on this theme involves assuming causal relationships without supporting evidence. For example, if a passage tells you that Kristen broke her bicycle *and* that Kristen went to the store yesterday, then one answer choice might say that Kristen went to the store *to* buy a new bicycle. This could be correct if there's textual evidence to back it up: "Because she broke her bicycle, Kristen took a trip to the store" strongly suggests causality. Otherwise, *even if a cause-and-effect relationship seems reasonable to you*, you can't assume characters' motivations unless there's textual evidence to support them.

False Case 3: The passage *suggests* an idea or conclusion, but an answer choice states it as fact (or vice versa, but more often not). This is especially common in, but certainly is not limited to, the science passages. Say, for instance, a passage states, "Dr. Kim and his team believe that this new vaccine could putatively bring about an end to HIV transmission in humans," (suggestion) and an answer choice says, "Dr. Kim's team discovered a vaccine that prevents HIV" (statement of fact). These aren't compatible. Look out for words like putatively, arguably, seemingly, apparently, ostensibly, possibly, potentially, hypothetically, hopefully, could, might, believe, expect, and predict. These all communicate that something *could* be true, but you don't know for sure.

True Wrong Answers

True, but irrelevant: The passage provides explicit evidence for an answer, but that answer choice does not actually answer the question. This is especially common for the "Which of the following provides the best evidence for the answer to the previous question?" question pairs. Often, you'll find that a piece of text from an answer to the second question (the "evidence" question) supports an answer to the first question, but that doesn't necessarily mean that the pair of answers is correct. Consider the following set of questions and possible answers:

1. Why was Catherine angry with Margot?
    - In 1851, Catherine's mother stole a fish from Benny.

2. Which of the following provides the best evidence for the answer to the previous question?
    - Lines 31-33 ("Of course, old Benny would never forget Catherine's mom's theft: way back in 1851, she took from him his only salmon!")

Here, the answer choice for Question 2 proves that the corresponding answer choice to Question 1 is *true*, but it doesn't (at least not in my made-up story) explain why Catherine is upset with Margot. These are super pesky combinations of answers, and they trick students all the time. *Just because an answer choice is true doesn't mean it's correct.* Make sure to answer the question above all else. As always, an easy way to avoid making this kind of mistake is to read all the answer choices and the questions very clearly. One extremely common mistake is to assume that any question that has quotes with line numbers in the answer choices must be linked to the previous question (i.e., it must be a "Which of the following provides the best evidence for the answer to the previous question?" question). That's not always the case. Be careful.

True, but not supported by the passage: An answer choice is (or would reasonably seem) true, but there's no way to know it based on the passage. Consider a passage that outlines an experiment conducted on a group of pigeons. Nowhere does the passage mention DNA or, for that matter, any chemicals, but an answer to one of the questions says, "Adenine most often pairs with thymine in DNA." This answer is absolutely true, but if the passage doesn't support it (explicitly or implicitly—as in the passage hints at or alludes to this fact), then the answer is wrong, even if this true but unsupported answer choice would reasonably answer the question.

As you're going over your missed and misunderstood questions for each practice exam, see if you can identify why each wrong answer is indeed wrong—in other words, which category of wrong it belongs to. If you find yourself struggling with this task, then the College Board's official SAT practice test explanations will lead you in the right direction. Remember, there's no such thing as a good wrong answer. Answers on the SAT are either right or wrong; there's nothing in between.

2. Why is the right answer right?

Because of the strict dichotomy between answers (they're either right or wrong), if you're proficient at identifying wrong answers, then you're by definition proficient at identifying right answers. If it's not wrong, it's right. Right answers belong to the SAT Holy Trinity: true, supported by textual evidence from the passage, and relevant to the question. One last time, don't automatically assume that an apparently good answer is the right answer. Scrutinize all the answer choices before deciding which one is correct. You have plenty of time on the SAT reading exam, so evaluate all your options. The people who write the exam absolutely try to trick you into choosing "trap" answers: the true and irrelevant or true but not supported by evidence answers. Read everything.

3. Why did I get it wrong?

This is by leaps and bounds the most important of The Big Three. Master the skills and concepts I introduce to you in the rest of this chapter, and you'll master the SAT reading exam. For each question, once you've figured out why all the wrong answers are wrong and the right answer is right (again, using the official College Board explanations helps a ton with this), you have to figure out what went wrong with your strategy and approach. Simply identifying what you did wrong is not enough. Just a casual "Oh, I get it" changes nothing. Get knocked down, get back up, and *change something*. I've found that just as wrong answers inevitably fall into just a few categories, so too do wrong problem-solving strategies. For every question that you missed or didn't understand, you need to diagnose your strategic mistake and figure out how to fix it: Do you need to invest more time into practicing vocabulary? Into reviewing the structure of science passages? Into paying more attention to detail? Into maintaining stronger and clearer focus?

Read this section and Chapter Five like self-help guides because that's what they are. As you go through them, you'll find yourself going, "Yup! Das me! I do that all the time." Excellent—we've identified problems. Then read over my suggestions to improve and write down a new strategy or study habit that you'll try next time. No matter how much you want to improve, you aren't going to remember all the mistakes you've made and all the ways to avoid those mistakes on your next exam. Keep a list and write everything down. (I said write it down, not type it onto your phone or computer.)

Then, before you jump back into reading your daily articles, look over your list. What are a few weaknesses you'd like to target? Say them out loud and be very clear with yourself what your goal for your reading practice is. Don't just read for the sake of reading—and don't take practice exams just for the sake of taking practice exams. Give purpose to your practice. Working harder doesn't necessarily lead to improvement or success. Working smarter, however, will lead to some real results. You're here to raise your score and get into your dream school, not to slave away and give all your good youthful years to the College Board.

To that end, try new things and keep an open mind. If I suggest that you write a brief summary for each paragraph you read, please do so. If I recommend that you start listening to a certain podcast or read a specific book, then give it a try. I'm not merely suggesting remedies because I have the homeopathic pipedream that they'll help you. I'm giving you tips and nibbles of advice that natural selection (i.e., watching the effects on my students' performance over the past decade) has honed for your benefit. If one of my suggestions sounds funny or a little crazy to you, then rest assured it sounds funny and crazy to me too—but if it gets you closer to a perfect score, who cares how outlandish it sounds? We're in this together, and if your current SAT prep regimen isn't getting you the score you want, then you have to make some changes.

Your concerns will fall into one of the following excuse categories:

- "I made a silly mistake."
- "I didn't have enough time."
- "I didn't know what that one word meant."
- "I didn't understand what the passage was saying."
- "I didn't recognize the author's attitude."

Pinpoint your issue on a per-question basis. You might find you have the same problem for five questions, or you might have five questions each with a different cause to improve. Notice that I called these excuses. It's all about your outlook and whether you're honest about your performance. Stop making excuses and start making improvements. For each question, 1) identify your excuse, 2) translate it to an honest explanation, and 3) find a solution. Target the mistakes you tend to make most often: if you never run out of time, then don't spend the bulk of your practice routine focusing on the "I ran out of time" section.

"I made a silly mistake."

I told you before that there's no such thing as a "silly mistake," and I meant it. Mistakes are real, and they're due to lack of knowledge and skill, but *silly* mistakes don't exist. My concern with silly mistakes is that they give you a false sense of security. When you say you just made a silly mistake, you tell yourself that you don't need to change your strategy, that you only got a question wrong by chance, as though the stochastic powers that be were out to get you and only you on that question. That's a lie, and it's a lazy one.

Here's another really aggravating nugget of "wisdom" I've heard from many SAT teachers and tutors: "The difference between a 1500 and a 1600 is just luck." What they mean is that you can prepare and garner the skills necessary to get to the 1500 level, but after that it's just luck of the draw. In other words, the students who get a 1600 just so *happened* to randomly be more focused, analytical, and careful on test day. That's not at all how it works.

Let's put this into some perspective. At the 2012 Olympics, Michael Phelps won the gold medal for the men's 100m butterfly. Phelps beat the silver medalists (there was a tie for second place) by 0.23 seconds. He also won the men's 200m individual relay by just 0.63 seconds and won two other gold medals—by similarly tiny margins—in team relay races. One could argue that Phelps struck gold (pun intended) by sheer luck, that his training and preparation got him to a high level, but his first-place finishes ultimately came down to afflatus. Nonsense. In 2012, Michael Phelps was the greatest swimmer in the world: he was better, stronger, and faster than everyone else, not because of chance but because of intense prep. If he had a weakness, he trained to combat it. Those mere

> *There's no such thing as a "silly mistake."*

fractions of seconds were the products of excruciatingly diligent practice, not divine intervention or random chance. His competitors didn't lose to him because they made "silly mistakes." Phelps was just better.

Similarly, perfect-scorers on the SAT don't get lucky on exam day. They're just better prepared for the test. By the way, "better prepared" doesn't mean "better at taking the SAT." It means they're more analytical, have stronger vocabularies, and are more experienced readers. This should resonate as extremely motivating: you are in complete control of your SAT destiny. What leads you to make "silly mistakes" that perfect-scorers don't? Lack of focus and practice-refined skill. If you tell yourself you made a mistake by chance, you're lying to yourself… and holding yourself back from the perfect score you absolutely can achieve.

The "I just made a silly mistake" excuse has a few slimy aliases: "I didn't see the NOT," "I didn't see that detail, but I see it now," and worst of all, "I got it right but bubbled the wrong answer choice." My heart stops when I hear students say these, especially the last one, which is such a blatant lie. You either bubbled the wrong answer choice or you got the question right—it's totally impossible to do both. There's no partial credit. The College Board and the universities you'll apply to don't care if you knew the right answer but didn't choose it.

Okay, enough of my interrogating, "What do you mean you didn't see the NOT!? It's in bold and all caps!" What we care most about is how to ensure you *do* see the NOTs, you *do* see relevant details, and you *don't* mistakenly bubble wrong answer choices in the future.

The chief reason that students make these mistakes is that they lack or lose focus during the exam. Often, this is because they prioritize speed over accuracy and blaze through the passages, the questions, and the answers without giving themselves enough time to process what's being said or asked. Other times, lack of focus stems from boredom: "And then Gregory surreptitiously absconded from the venue, unaware that his *blah blah blah… yawn! Can this story be over already!?*" Finally, lack of focus can result from an outright physiological inability to focus.

If you think that you may have a medical inability to focus, then jump ahead to Page 119. Attention deficit can seriously limit your ability to succeed in academia, so take it seriously.

I discussed focus back in Chapter Two (Page 39), and if you find yourself losing focus often (and thus making "silly mistakes"), then I strongly recommend that you go back and reread what I briefly said there before continuing with this section.

Telling yourself, "I'll be more focused next time," will not make you more focused next time. If you struggle to stay focused, then you must take intentional steps to hone your focus, and you must make building focus a core part of your practice routine.

Some students don't realize that focus is not a gift but a skill, so you can practice it, strengthen it, and nurture it. How many times in a given day would you say you focus on something for more than five uninterrupted minutes? I'd bet zero. Think of how many times you're distracted by your phone, your thoughts, or your senses.

Trying to pay close attention to your science teacher's lecture? Two minutes in and BZZZZ! A notification! *Did Sarah finally reply to my Snapchat?! Did someone retweet my joke?! Did I get the callback?!* "... And that's how to predict whether a substance is a solid, liquid, or gas at room temperature." *Who, wait, what now?*

Whether you're watching TV, taking an exam, enjoying a relaxing shower, or reading a good book, no matter how invested you are in the task at-hand, you most likely focus in very sporadic, bite-sized chunks, punctuated by equally frequent stretches of listless distraction. When you say, "I'm paying very close attention," you probably really mean, "I have no idea what's going on right now."

Let's start flexin' that focus muscle whenever possible. First things first, you need to minimize the number of distractions in your vicinity. I don't think you necessarily need to go on a digital detox and do away with all the devices you own (though it's definitely not a bad idea), but I do think that you should try at least a few of the following:

- During school, switch your phone to silent instead of vibrate. Better yet, keep your phone in your backpack. Sometimes you just *think* your phone vibrated, and that alone is enough to distract you, even if your phone's on silent or there's no notification awaiting you.

- Designate an hour of your day as "analog-only" time: no phone, no computer, no TV, no WiFi, no Bluetooth. There's nothing going on online that's more important than your own peace and tranquility.

- Download a meditation app and practice mindfulness. HeadSpace and Waking Up are two that I'd recommend. Every night, for just a few minutes, sit down somewhere comfortable, turn off your devices, close your eyes, and do absolutely nothing. Don't worry about the SAT or your classes or college apps. Don't think about that funny meme you saw last night. Let your thoughts come and let them go.

- Pick up a book and try to read through just one page without daydreaming or thinking of *anything* other than what's on that page. This is harder than you'd think! If you get distracted halfway through, start over. Then graduate to two, three, five pages at a time.

- Exercise or start doing yoga. You can find plenty of relaxing exercise and yoga videos on YouTube. I'm partial to XHit's Five Minute Abs.

- The next time you feel bored, stay bored for a little while. Instead of immediately trying to supplant your boredom with an activity (or your Instagram feed), *relish* in your boredom. Embrace your boredom. "Just sitting here doing nothing is so boring!" you'll say. That's okay. It's okay to be bored. I bet you our caveman ancestors were pretty darn bored most of the time. Even if you just pause for a minute (literally count to 60 if you have to) of nothing before you find something to do, you turn boredom into that much less of a bogeyman—you train your brain to welcome boredom instead of receding into fear and anxiety whenever boredom looms. Time passes a lot more slowly than you think, and if you spend your whole life doing things just to prevent boredom, then how boring is that?

These are all things you can do with very little effort and with very great reward. In just a few weeks, you'll be amazed at how much you can rewire your brain. When you go to take your next practice exam, remind yourself beforehand to slow down, read carefully, and completely read questions before you try to answer them. You have the ability to stay focused, and you definitely won't be making any more "silly mistakes."

"I didn't have enough time."

"I didn't have enough time" could really mean a few things: you're reading too slow, you're reading too fast, you're spending too much time on individual questions, or you're losing focus.

Take a reading speed test online to find out how fast you read. If you find that your reading speed is lower than around 100 words per minute, then you're on the slower side (most of you can probably *type* at that speed). That's okay, but it does mean that you need to allocate more time during the day to reading. Don't tell yourself you need to—or can—double your reading speed overnight. Make gradual progress and read at a pace that's comfortable to you. Back when you were learning your times tables, you started out slow and worked your way up to doing them rapidly. Set reasonable expectations.

If you find that your reading speed is much higher than 225 or so words per minute, then you might be reading a bit too fast, which can end up actually costing you time instead of saving it. There's an old quote from Woody Allen that succinctly captures this conundrum: "I took a speed reading course and read *War and Peace* in twenty minutes. It involves Russia." Just because your eyes look at all the words on a page doesn't mean you've read anything.

I can tell you that my eyes have seen every single word of *The Odyssey*, but I couldn't tell you one thing that happens along Odysseus's journey except that he shoots a bow and arrow at some point and uses sheep to hide from a cyclops (and I only remember those things because

I read them on Shmoop). If you hurriedly blaze through a passage to try and save thirty seconds of reading but then have to spend an extra five minutes struggling through the questions because you don't remember anything you read, then you're wasting time. Pro-tip: don't waste time. There's no gold star awaiting whoever finishes the exam fastest, but there's a bevy of college admissions and scholarships that awaits whoever gets the most questions correct. Slow down and read carefully the first time through.

Perhaps it's not reading the passages but answering the questions that's taking up an inordinate amount of your time. I went over this earlier in the "Lacking confidence" section of Chapter One (Page 45), so if you find yourself often spending more than at most a minute on a question, then I'd recommend you reread that section before moving forward. You have to constantly remind yourself that the SAT asks you rather simple and straightforward questions. Consequently, spending more than a minute on any question is a clear sign that you're overthinking. One student told me he spent ten minutes on just one question early in his reading exam—and then had to guess on the last fifteen. !?!?!? If you struggle on one or two questions, so be it; don't bring down a dozen others in the process. Part of being a confident test-taker is knowing that if a question is hard for you, then it's probably hard for many other test-takers as well. Remain calm, cool, and collected.

Often the reason you'll spend such a long time on a question is that you simply can't find textual evidence to support an answer. Slow down and pay better attention as you're reading. That way, when the questions refer to a particular event or idea from the passage, you'll reliably be able to remember where it came up. Better yet, skim the questions before you read the passage. It's much harder to overlook key details the first time when you know exactly what you're looking for.

Finally, if you lose focus, then you lose time. At this point, you should know what to do if you're losing time due to lack of focus. (If not, see Page 94.)

"I didn't know what that one word meant."

Sometimes one word is enough to completely trip you up. Learn the word, accept that your vocabulary has room to grow, and keep on trucking. If you find yourself up against a word whose definition you could never in a million years figure out without looking it up, then narrow down your answer choices as best you can based on the wrong answer categories we've already discussed, guess, and move on. You'll be just fine. One question won't be near enough to bring you down. Make vocabulary that much more of a priority during your reading.

"I didn't understand what the passage was saying."

If you knew all the vocabulary in a passage and read at a proper pace but still couldn't figure out what the author was trying to say (this is a problem that students most often have on the social/science passages), then you probably need to reevaluate your understanding of argumentative writing structure.

You hopefully know how to write a proper essay, and you hopefully know all the components that go into strong writing: clear and relevant background information, a well-defined and arguable thesis, direct topic sentences and supporting evidence, and a summative conclusion that connects to a broader idea. Surprise! The passages (aside from the first one) follow this same flow. Keep a mental checklist and be on the constant lookout for these elements in each passage.

If you aren't too strong on argumentation and essay writing, then look into the Toulmin model for building an argument. Toulmin outlines six components required for crafting a sound argument, and you want to look out for these in any argumentative writing that you read. Put yourself in the author's shoes. If you were writing, how would you support your argument? What would you use as evidence? How would you clarify your attitude to your readers? Review the "New People Talking

About Politics and Society" and "Summaries of Science Experiments or Studies" portions of Chapter Three (Page 72) for more guidance as well. The worksheets I've provided you for those passages also indicate which key elements you ought to be paying attention to and actively looking for.

"I didn't recognize the author's attitude."

This really means your vocabulary is lacking. Remember, vocabulary isn't just about denotations (dictionary definitions)—it's also about connotations. Consider the difference between "I am displeased with you" and "I am pissed off at you." "I am displeased" suggests an air of disappointment, of unmet expectations, whereas "I am pissed off" means blood is boiling and hands are about to be thrown. Similarly, "I was taken aback by the *stench* of his room" and "I was taken aback by the *fragrance* of his room" are completely different statements. Even though "stench" and "fragrance" both mean "smell," a fragrance makes me wistfully smile, while a stench makes me want to vomit. So, if you find yourself at a loss for authors' attitudes (tone), then double down on your vocabulary and try listening to a narration (an audiobook) while you read. When you can hear the way an author pronounces the text, it's far tougher to misinterpret tone, and you'll develop a more tonally accurate reading voice of your own.[6]

Sometimes you can't recognize when an author is being sarcastic. Translation: You don't have a sense of humor. I'm kidding. Sorta. Sarcasm is occasionally difficult to discern, and humor definitely takes a bit of getting used to. Even then, it's far more difficult to recognize sarcasm in print than in speech or visual media. Without the luxury of vocal tonal inflection, how can you possibly know when an author is being

---

6 By "reading voice" I mean the voice in your head that you hear as you read and write: your subvocalization.

humorous, sarcastic, or sardonic? Well, you just do (or, apparently, don't). The best way to familiarize yourself with sarcasm is to read Mark Twain and watch the comedy of Stephen Colbert, Jon Stewart, or George Carlin. Watch *Friends*, *Saturday Night Live*, *Last Week Tonight with John Oliver*, and other television comedies where you can hear the audience's laughter. That way, you can recognize sarcastic or comical sentence structures and styles of speech. You'll catch on quickly, and the SAT only rarely asks you to identify sarcasm anyways.

One thing to look out for is italics that indicate sarcasm. Think about the difference between "You forgot your keys, didn't you?" and "You forgot your keys, *didn't* you?" The second is more abrasive and caustic—you can almost hear the insult that would likely follow. Authors sometimes rely on italics to communicate sarcasm, but, to be clear, italics don't *only* indicate sarcasm. The italicized "only" in the previous sentence is for emphasis but certainly not for any comedic effect.

Every time you go through a practice exam, revisit this chapter as needed to reassess the types of mistakes you're making and what you can change so that you don't make those mistakes again. With time and practice, you'll have all the skills and knowledge you need for a perfect reading score. Now, I know that it will get tough along the way. You might question whether you're legitimately improving or why you should even care about your SAT score at all. The next chapter is for your inspiration. Think of it as chicken noodle soup for the test-taker's soul. We all fall into slumps. We get excited and enthusiastic about studying—only to burn out a few days later because the results we want aren't coming fast enough. When this happens, reread Chapter Five!

CHAPTER FIVE

What's It All For?

There is only one commonality between the learning habits of all students: everyone hits many, many road blocks along the way to success. For some of us, that means a physiological inability to focus (perhaps caused by a deficit in serotonin and norepinephrine in the brain). For others, that means running into bouts of insecurity or lack of motivation. For still others, that means tripping over ontological questions of the form "Does my score even matter?" and "Is the SAT even real?"

The purpose of this chapter is to give you an emotional boost whenever you encounter one of these success deterrents. Some of you may find it helpful to read over sections of this chapter once every few weeks, while others of you may find yourself needing support every night—or somewhere in between. For all of you, it's most important that you know that it's okay to stumble. Like we've examined before, everyone experiences setbacks, but how you change your habits in response to those setbacks determines your success. Chapter Four taught you how to respond to the mistakes you make on practice exams. This chapter teaches you how to stay motivated and respond to broader studying concerns, for the SAT and beyond. In other words, what's it all for?

This chapter is a sequence of concerns and questions that students most often pose or ask when studying. Read over them all at least once and, when needed, return to those that pertain to you.

I just don't want to study.

Trust me, you aren't alone. Sometimes, I don't want to do anything at all… much less something productive. I couldn't begin to tell you the number of times that, while writing this book, I wanted to throw my laptop at the wall and give up because I was so unmotivated to finish. *I just don't wanna!* And with so many readily available alternatives (I can open up Netflix or Hulu by pressing just one button on my remote—*one button!*), it's no wonder we find it so insanely difficult to stay productive.

Indeed, given that tech giants like Facebook, Snapchat, Google, YouTube, and Netflix spend outrageous eight-figure sums of cash every year to make their platforms as addictive as possible, you should be amazed that you manage to get *anything* done.

Here's the deal: no one wants to study. Nobody wakes up in the morning, stretches out his arms, takes in a deep breath, and shouts, "Hooray! Study time!" You might argue that researchers who enjoy their vocation clearly enjoy studying. Nope. Researchers don't study; researchers research. Journalists research. Authors, historians, artists, and public speakers research, but they don't study.

Research is exciting, cavernous, unpredictable, and serendipitous. It's uncovering an interesting fact or datum and then exploring the medical, social, economic, and political ramifications thereof. Research is pushing the bounds of human knowledge and discovering information heretofore unknown to any living being—and some people get so hooked on this phenomenon that they devote their entire lives to research.

Studying is the bastard child of research. When you're studying, you're just memorizing the results of someone else's research. You don't ask why or how we know DNA is a double helix; you just kinda accept it and pray you can answer questions about it on an exam. Of course, the reason for this is plain: you likely know next to nothing about x-ray crystallography or nuclear magnetic resonance (NMR)—among other techniques to identify molecular structure—so you have to take your biology textbook at face value and trust that Watson and Crick knew what they were talking about. That's boring.

Even so, a small fraction of you—probably, the ones of you who will likely pursue chemistry, biology, or medicine in the future—just put down this book and typed "NMR" or "crystallography" into Google, and perhaps you got lost in a sea of YouTube videos or science articles that outline how we use some pretty advanced technologies to determine the structure of complex molecules. That's research: using new information as a springboard to investigate new frontiers in your knowledge and insight. That's exciting.

But studying is boring. It's just the rote means to the end of high test scores. We're all *researchers* at heart. Why do we binge watch an entire series on Netflix? Because we want to know what happens in the lives of the characters. Who dies? Who gets married? Who gets the final rose? How does Aang ultimately defeat Ozai? Do Rachel and Ross finally end up together? Sure, television is entertaining, but it's entertaining because we have an intrinsic drive to find out what happens next.

No one wants to study.

Well-produced television explores the backstories and emotional states of characters and their relationships; the more we understand, the more attached and invested we become, the more we want to discover. Is that not research?

The same goes for video games. No doubt, part of their allure is (if you play MMOs) the camaraderie with friends, but even video games are just laboratories for research. The fact that you can train, hone skills, and better predict outcomes makes video games addictive. *What if we go off-meta? What if I try this chassis/engine combo? What if I try a hitch instead of a go route?* It's all experimentation. That's also why you'll spend three hours on YouTube looking at different makeup tutorials, tech reviews, documentaries, music videos, comedy sketches, or interviews. Every video is a point of departure for the next: *I liked that camera model, now let me learn about another so I can compare them.* Research is addicting, and it's really fun.

Textbooks? Boring! Okay, great, the Stamp Act was passed in 1765—I'll do my best to remember that for the exam; now back to *Black Panther.* Novels written so long ago that it's hard to say for sure that they're even in English? Boring! If it's just memorizing facts, then it's studying. If you can't understand material well enough that it inspires further lines of inquiry, then it's just studying. And studying sucks.

The trick, then, is to turn studying into research whenever possible and practical—and reasonable. For some things, it's just not worth it. If you find yourself descending so far down the rabbit hole of research that you begin to question why $7 + 2 = 9$, then you've gone astray. Don't turn into one of those people who hears someone say, "The sky is blue," and feverishly retorts, "Is it really, though? What even is blue? Where do you draw the line? Is it still blue at night? What if you're color blind? Is it still blue if no one ever looks at it?" Go home, Felicia. Save those questions for your PhD dissertation where they belong.

In other words, sometimes you're stuck with studying and need to get over yourself. Just do it.

So, here's some inspiration for studying: everything you can learn by studying is only studiable because the entire pantheon of human knowledge and research has made it so. Take, for example, a history textbook. Historians pore over thousands of years' worth of artifacts, texts, scientific data, language, and culture to substantiate what might end up in about two pages of your average high-school history textbook. Further, none of that information would even exist without language and culture to begin with, which our ancestors have handed down over many tens of thousands of years. Our languages, our stories, and our histories have survived ice ages and world wars, tsunamis and volcanic eruptions, pandemics and genocides. Indeed, all that remains of everyone who has ever lived and died is information; when we study, we tap into the rich legacy that the thinkers, doers, and revolutionaries of our species left behind for us. That's pretty cool.

Think about this. Even the notion that 7 + 2 = 9 isn't an obvious one. Ask a chimp to do addition and subtraction and see how far it gets. Our ability to memorize and understand even the most basic of concepts is only possible because our ancestors did the research and philosophizing that turned what was then groundbreaking into what is today preschool math. Studying may be boring, but it's a privilege, and we would all do well to pay our forebears a little bit more respect here and there by studying more committedly and more enthusiastically.[1]

That said, we can often transform studying opportunities into research opportunities—a worthwhile and adventurous pursuit. The easiest way to do this is to turn your studies (perhaps, the study guides that your teachers provide) into Wikipedia sprees.[2] If you want to know more about, say, aniline dyes, you could navigate to the Wikipedia article "Aniline." Available to you then is not only a laundry list of facts about aniline, but also a swath of links to other related topics: fuchsine, vanadium, Nikolay Zinin, and African sleeping sickness, just to name a small few. You may find that you're not initially all that interested in aniline, but African sleeping sickness may sound a lot more worth your time. From

> *Studying may be boring, but it's a privilege.*

---

1 If you commiserate with this perspective, or if you enjoy great books, I highly recommend Steven Pinker's eye-opening *Enlightenment Now*. Pinker expands on my position and makes clear why our ability to think and create is so precious.

2 Many of you have likely heard from your teachers that Wikipedia is not a good or reliable source for research. Ten years ago that was true, but in the decade(s) since your teachers graduated college, Wikipedia has become one of the most accurate resources available, and your teachers are just bitter that they didn't have it when they were in school back in the Dark Ages.

the "African trypanosomiasis" (sleeping sickness) article, you may find yourself gravitating toward the "Tsetse fly" page, then to "Theodore Roosevelt," and finally to "Income tax in the United States." Of course, if you need to know basic information about aniline, commit yourself to memorizing that information for whatever it is you're studying. But also let yourself drift: "That sounds interesting. Let me find out more!" are the sweetest words in the English language.

My friends and I used to have "Wikipedia races" in our spare time. We'd each discreetly pick a Wikipedia page, and we'd see who could get from one to the other in the shortest amount of time only by clicking links on each page. Try it sometime! It's a fun way to practice your ability to make connections between ideas and information. See how many clicks it takes you to get from "George Washington" to "Electric guitar."

The hallmark of research is that an investigator often discovers something he or she didn't initially expect or set out to find. Allow yourself the flexibility to explore new ideas that you aren't being tested on; develop your intellectual curiosity. If you're studying Thomas Jefferson, go and read some of the letters he wrote to Sally Hemings. It's much more interesting to study the sultry improprieties of historical figures than to try and remember the years they were born. Maybe you're learning about vectors in math. Who developed the concept of vectors? From where did the concept of a vector "cross product" originate? How are vectors useful in other fields like chemistry and physics?

These questions reveal the final problems with studying: nearly everything we're forced to memorize lacks context and applicability— and it's almost always watered down and simplified. As you should now realize, this is fundamentally at odds with your instinct to explore. When presented in textbooks and other study materials, subjects seem finite, as though if something's not in the textbook, it doesn't exist. I told a student some years ago about a class, which I took in college, called Nucleic Acid Biochemistry. "There's a whole class on that?!" he responded, apparently astounded. Because his biology textbook spends a single chapter on DNA, he didn't think there was any more to know about nucleic acids than what was in that chapter. What we learn in high school is exceptionally limited, and the more aware of this we are, the better.

Sometimes this limitation is necessary and helpful. In physics, for example, most equations make little to no sense without their calculus-based derivations. So, for a physics student who's still in algebra 2, it's reasonable to just memorize equations without understanding where they come from.[3] Many students, though, see this veil between "what" and "why" as opaque: they think that high school physics is the pinnacle of physics. They think that geology is no more complicated than the earth science they learned in elementary school. This dangerously inaccurate perspective limits their potential for academic growth by poisoning their research instincts, leading to mental dystrophy.

If you find yourself, then, asking "Will I ever use this?" or "It's that simple?" then do some further research. Peruse Wikipedia, take an online college course, or check out a higher-level text from your library. The more you know, the more connections between ideas you can forge (academia has recently come to the realization that interdisciplinary research

> *If you tell yourself nothing is out there, that's all you'll find.*

often bears more fruit than myopic, unidisciplinary research), and the more excited you'll become about your studies. If you tell yourself nothing is out there, that's all you'll find.

I haven't forgotten about the SAT—and at this point you might be wondering whether everything I've just said can help encourage you to study for the reading exam. Without question it can and should.

---

3 Daniel C. Dennett, in *From Bacteria to Bach and Back*, refers to this as "competence without comprehension." In some cases, it's okay to know *how* to do something without knowing *why it works*. For example, you likely don't know why the plural form of "goose" is "geese," but you know how to use it in a sentence, and that's just fine.

When you begin to view vocabulary as a window into the linguistic history of our species, it becomes a far more exciting pursuit. Words aren't just words; they're vectors for ideas, the tools we use to change hearts and minds. The greater your vocabulary, the stronger your ability to influence the world—and to get a perfect SAT reading score.

When you begin to see reading passages as opportunities for research (and sources of inspiration for Wikipedia races!), you'll never again have to force yourself to read. Countless generations and lifetimes have made your reading possible: it's a privilege, not a responsibility.

The next time you find yourself unwilling to study, give this section another look-over. Your brain is the culmination of billions—with a b!—of years of natural selection, and you've only got the one. Use it wisely and set it free. *Studying* is boring, but *research* is as primal and instinctual as breathing, and you never have to force yourself to breathe.

I don't have enough time to study.

Yes, you do. A popular joke among high school students is that between good grades, enough sleep, and a social life, you're allowed to pick two. So powerful has this meme become that it's infected the minds of every student I've ever worked with.[4] It's absolute self-fulfilling nonsense, and we need to put it to an end right now.

I know that many of you truly are extremely busy. Between sports, theater, volunteering, internships, coursework, family responsibilities, band, and every other extracurricular, you've probably got plenty on your plate even without SAT prep. High school is one of the busiest and most demanding times—and after graduation some of you might never again find yourselves as busy as you are now. But we all know the tea is that you

---

4 This probably seems like an inappropriately epidemiological way to phrase this, but memes *are* infectious; they just spread from mind to mind, while a viral or bacterial infection spreads from body to body. It's still infection. More on this in Chapter Six.

find plenty of time for completely unproductive activities, time that you could instead invest in your progress toward mastering the SAT.

Whatever your poison of choice—be it social media, video games, television, or that more lascivious corner of the internet (or, most likely, all of the above)—moderation is key. One game of League of Legends here and there isn't going to keep you from academic success, but five games a night certainly will. If you find yourself in a bitter uphill battle against a tech addiction, then don't try to quit cold turkey. Slowly wean yourself off, and gradually replace your bad habits with good ones like studying, exercise, and meditation. It's more than okay to take a break from the constant onslaught of high-school responsibilities. In fact, you'd probably go crazy if you didn't take breaks and veg out on a TV show every once in a while. But instead of watching eight episodes in a row, just watch one and save the next for later. Instead of watching eighteen YouTube videos, settle for just a couple. Nothing interesting is happening on Facebook, Instagram, or Twitter on a high-school Wednesday night. Finish your work first, and all the pictures and tweets you could ever want will be there later, too.

Aside from social media, TV, and video games, another huge time suck for high school students (and people in general) is simply worrying about how much time they have. How many times have you written out a list both of your responsibilities and of when you want to accomplish them... only to find yourself so fraught with anxiety that you accomplished nothing but watching yet another episode of *The Office*? Yeah, me too. When you waste time thinking about how long all your tasks are going to take, you psych yourself out and give your responsibilities way more power over you than they deserve.

If you've got work to do, then just do it. Don't let your agenda stress you out. Do what you can and don't worry more about planning your work than doing your work. When you get home each day, grab a bite to eat, take a shower, and do nothing for a little while. "Do nothing" doesn't mean go on Instagram and neglect your responsibilities—it means nothing. Meditate for a good five or ten minutes. Then, get to work. After every forty-five minutes of work, get up, stretch, and dive into another five minutes of meditation. Throughout, if your mind starts to drift or worry about all the other assignments you're going to have to finish after the one you're currently working on, take back control by meditating yet again—even if just for a minute (as I've told you before, literally count to 60 if you have to). Then repeat, and you'll discover that your schoolwork isn't that tough or time-consuming after all! Stick with problems, ask questions, seek help when needed, and don't give up.

When you go into your schoolwork and other responsibilities with the confidence that you are capable of producing high-quality work and not wasting time, you will produce high-quality work and not waste time. Prove to yourself that you are willing and able to commit to developing positive, success-making habits.

You have as much time as you'll let yourself have. You can get good grades, maintain a positive social life, and sleep on time every day, but only if you are honest. Oh, how many times I've heard students say, "I studied five hours for that exam," only to later discover they really spent twenty minutes simply worrying about the exam and the remaining two-hundred-eighty minutes on social media—even when studying for just a half-hour would have gotten them an A. You have as much time as you'll let yourself have. So, let yourself have as much time to study or to prepare for the SAT as you need. Everything else can come later.

Studying for the SAT isn't exciting.
(Or: Do I even want to go to college?")

Let's start with a super easy-to-answer, simple, totally inconsequential question: What do you want in life? Get out a pen and paper and write down five things you really, really want for yourself. Maybe you really want to take a special someone to the next big school dance, or maybe you wish you could roll up to school in a G-Wagen.

Perhaps you want nothing more than to prove wrong everyone who's ever doubted you by printing out a giant copy of your Harvard acceptance letter and parading it around town. What would fill you up with some pure unadulterated joy?

If goals like "Get an A on my next math test" or "Improve my SAT score" are on your list, then you're thinking way too small and way too academic. Go bigger picture: where do you want to see yourself a year from now? Ten years from now? That *isn't* the same as "Where do you see yourself ten years from now?" Your I-want statements should have no bounds. The more you limit what you desire, the more you limit what you can accomplish. If you can't dream it, you'll absolutely never do it.

Now figure out where the SAT fits into that list. If you find yourself thinking that the best path to success for you is to obtain a bachelor's degree from Stanford, then the SAT obviously fits very squarely into your dreams—and, by extension, it turns out that you actually *do* want to study for the SAT! It very well may be the case, however, that your goals are entirely unacademic, and that's more than okay.[5] Perhaps, for example, your goal is to market a YouTube channel that delivers comedy content to high-school students, and you foresee a large enough following that you could financially support yourself with ad revenue. By all means, if you have the passion, likeability, and talent, don't let anyone stop you from accomplishing that!

Whatever the case, honesty is what matters most. I firmly believe that unrelenting dedication and passion are unstoppable forces toward success. That said, life does happen. If your goal is to become a professional athlete, then one injury could end your career in a painful

---

5 Famously, Robert Kiyosaki's *Rich Dad Poor Dad* outlines how the erroneous meme that studying determines financial success has taken near unshakeable hold of the working middle class. Schools are effectively factories for producing college professors (see Ken Robinson's TED Talk "Do Schools Kill Creativity?"). Not all of us want to be college professors, and some of us don't need much formal academic training at all to be successful. Just be honest with yourself about what it is you want to be and the road there.

instant. Figure out what contingencies could hold you back. Dedication won't turn you into a pro football player if you can't walk. Always give yourself options, and always have a backup (preferably have multiple backups). If you want the stability and confidence to know that, should you become physically unable to reach your dreams, you'll still be able to pursue academia, then the SAT still fits into your plans.

I had a friend in high school whose dream was to become an Air Force pilot. He spent many years preparing for the Air Force Academy, got rejected, worked hard, got accepted, and later found out that his depth perception wasn't strong enough to qualify him for flying. So, instead of giving up, he doubled down on his studies and got degrees in philosophy and history. His SAT score doubtless helped him get into college when he had to leave the Academy. He didn't immediately benefit from SAT prep right out of high school, but his prep sure paid off down the road. He had options.

Also keep in mind where the job market is moving. What skills will our economy value in 2030? Will critical reading and analysis be marketable in ten years when robots can outperform us in nearly all physical tasks? (Yes.) Will a college degree still carry weight in the future economy? Maybe it will, and maybe it won't. Most big tech companies today, for instance, care far more about your technical experience than your academic résumé. With so many online academies and tutorials, it's never been easier to learn new valuable skills, so maybe you don't and won't need a degree to prove your worth.

Then again, as more and more workers are displaced from their labor-intensive jobs, they'll be competing against you, and they have access to all the online resources that you do. Bearing that in mind, a college degree—which tells employers that you have the wherewithal to endure four years of (often meaningless) assignments, to manage your time, to balance a social life, and to learn material that isn't directly related to your major—might become more valuable than ever in the field of job applicants, all else equal. So, the SAT again emerges as a powerful asset:

a high SAT score gives you more options and will help open more doors, even if you never end up needing to use them. That security is helpful.

When you find yourself bemoaning how studying isn't exciting, remind yourself that success *is* exciting, and you're preparing for the SAT and beyond to secure your future. Invest in yourself now because it will be much harder to do it later; ask any adults who have to take the SAT whether they're having an easy time prepping. (They're not.) The SAT is just a means to an end. Envision your goals, remind yourself that this puny exam is just a stepping stone to achieving those goals, and then get back to work!

My score is low.
(Or: My score is high.)

Is it? By what standard? Is 36% on an exam a low score? What if the mean is 24%, and the standard deviation is 2.6%? Now is it a low score? What if your teacher then decides that the cutoff for an A is 33% and that your 36% is an A+? Is it still a low score?

Students are all so used to the "90-100 is an A" grade scale that they apply it to the SAT as well. They're also so used to thinking about scores in terms of percentages that any other concept of scoring is foreign. Let's bring SAT scores into clearer focus.

When it comes to the SAT, percentage means absolutely nothing. The test is scaled from your raw score, and it's not meaningful to convert your scaled score to a percentage. What actually matters is your *percentile*, which tells you where you rank among all SAT test-takers. If you're in the 60th percentile, for example, then you performed at or above the level of 60% of all other test takers—even if you only got, say, 23% of the questions correct. Put another way, if you're in the 60th percentile, then you're in the top 40%. Similarly, if you're in the 90th percentile, then you're in the top 10%. Your percentile ranking tells you and tells colleges where you stack up against other applicants.

So, is a score of 1300, for example, a low score? By percentages you might think so. If you score 130/160 (81%) on an exam at school, you might be very disappointed with the B- you'd receive. (I recognize that some of you would be elated with a B-; I've been there.) But according to the College Board,[6] an SAT score of 1300 puts you in the 91st percentile of US high school juniors and seniors, and it puts you in the 87th percentile of all SAT test takers. In other words, a 1300—which many students see as a "low score"—actually means you're in the top 13% of all SAT test takers, which is pretty good. To put that into some perspective, the 87th percentile of individual income in the United States is $100,000 per year.[7] Your percentile means everything.

Before you decide that your score is low, talk with your college counselor and figure out which colleges you'll be applying to. Look at the data. What percentile of applicants do those schools generally accept? Do you need to be in the 50th, the 90th, or the 99th percentile? Compare your score with the scores of most accepted applicants (this data is available in many locations online—again, ask your college counselor for help), and *then* make a judgment call. Perhaps your score *is* very low considering the schools you want to apply to, but perhaps your score is, all things considered, dramatically higher than you thought.

In either case, your score is just a number—and it's only one of many, many factors that colleges will consider in the application process. Don't neglect your schoolwork and extracurriculars in the hopes that you'll boost your SAT score by ten points. That said, if your goal is to go to Yale but you're scoring a 1300 on the SAT, then instead of telling yourself that your score is low, see it as room to grow. It's just one exam, and I'm confident that if you put in the right work, you'll get the score you want!

---

6 www.collegereadiness.collegeboard.org/pdf/understanding-sat-scores.pdf

7 https://dqydj.com/income-percentile-calculator/

My score isn't improving.

You won't get your desired score by magic. Students often make small improvements and then stagnate for a while, before improving and stagnating again. One of the principal reasons for this is that students neglect to approach their SAT prep with intent. As I mentioned in Chapter Four, so many students get caught up in the useless loop of taking practice test after practice test, hoping that their scores will somehow go up. It's not gonna happen. If you get lazy and neglect to target your practice, you will not improve. Go back and reread Section 3 of Chapter Four (Page 92) and stick to the prescription I've provided.

It's altogether possible (of course) that you are adhering to my recommendations but still aren't managing to make progress. If your problem is that every exam trips you up with new vocabulary, then jump to the next section: "I suck at learning new vocabulary." If you've tried and tried and tried to stay focused but absolutely cannot—or if you have a medically-diagnosed attention deficit—jump to the section thereafter: "I actually cannot focus."

If neither applies to you, then it might be a good idea to seek the advice of an experienced tutor who can lead you in the right direction. You should seek a tutor who teaches you strategy, not content. Have someone examine the questions you're missing and ask him/her to design a study regimen that will help you target specific skills. It is absolutely not useful to have someone go through an entire exam with you and explain each question, as you will never see those questions again. You don't need to know how to answer those questions; you need to know what skills will help you answer similar questions next time (and those are two very different things, which many tutors find very difficult to comprehend).

If you can't find someone who can help or you feel you've hit a dead end in your SAT prep, you can always schedule a free consult with me at www.tutorjacob.com, and we can together figure out what your best plan of attack is.

I suck at learning new vocabulary.

If you've studied vocab the way I've suggested (see Page 33) but are still finding it difficult to remember new words, then take all of my recommendations to the next level.

Put bets on your ability. Bet a friend $10 that you'll be able to learn any ten words by the end of this week. Bet your parents or guardians that you'll learn twenty new words or else you won't be able to go out with friends over the weekend. Or bet for access to Netflix or to your computer or for a ride to school (if you live close enough to reasonably walk there). Would you be able to learn your words then?

Post words all on your luxuries at home. Every day, put new words on Post-Its on your computer, your deodorant, your mouthwash, your ice cream, your TV—whatever you (hopefully) want to use or consume—and don't let yourself use the item until you've learned the word on it. Have a friend change your social media passwords to new words: they'll give you a definition, and you'll have to figure out the new word to log into your accounts. Be creative!

Also, increase your exposure to new words by listening to academic or professional podcasts and watching television programs that draw on rich and topical vocabularies. That way, even when you're not studying, you'll still be studying! Some of my favorite podcasts are Making Sense with Sam Harris, Hidden Brain, What It Takes, No Such Thing As A Fish, and Twenty Thousand Hertz. Explore the podcasts that are out there and find something that entertains and excites you. On television or Netflix, watch serious dramas like *Sherlock*, *Breaking Bad*, *Downton Abbey*, and *Game of Thrones*. Different people speak in different styles and with different words and phrases, so the more sources of English you expose yourself to, the more reliable your ability to process text and speech without stumbling over unknown words.

You've learned tens of thousands of words in your lifetime. What's a few more?

I actually cannot focus.

If you've tried your absolute best to incorporate mindfulness and meditation into your studying routine for at least a month but can't seem to make any progress, it may be a good idea to consult with your school psychologist to discuss whether you could have a medically diagnosable attention deficit. Be honest about what constitutes "tried my absolute best." Using your phone for five fewer minutes for three days isn't trying your best to improve your focus. Make a concerted effort to change your habits and your dependency on your phone and computer. After that, seek guidance from a medical professional like a licensed therapist, school psychologist, or psychiatrist. If they suggest a diagnosis, take action.

If you have an attention deficit or anxiety that affects your test-taking speed, then the College Board might accommodate you, which could mean a world of difference. For more information, go to www.accommodations.collegeboard.org. If a professional—and it's always best to seek more than just one opinion—determines that you don't have a medical attention deficit, then you want to ramp up your focus practice: maybe join a yoga or meditation class, or look into a digital detox.

Nothing is more important than your health.

If you do have or get a diagnosis of an attention deficit, then don't be shy about requesting extra time from the SAT. Take advantage of the assistance that is available to you. That's advice that will go a long way in life no matter your circumstances. Even then, be aware that a psychobiological limitation is not prophecy. Yes, there are some of you who are genetically predisposed to lack focus, but that means your *range* of possible focus levels is lower. Within that range, you can and should still work hard to improve your focus level. No matter what, you're still in control!

I've got way bigger problems than the SAT.
(Or: I get depressed when I study for the SAT.)

Yes, you do. Like I've said before, no matter how hard we work or how dedicated we are, sometimes life happens and we have to reevaluate our priorities. When tragedy strikes, stay open to help. Seek the advice of trained professionals: social workers, psychologists, counselors, teachers, or psychiatrists. Available to you is a tremendous wealth of support and guidance, but it's most helpful if you take advantage of it. Prioritize your health (and that, of course, includes your mental health). If that means you have to take a year off from school, so be it. If that means you have to go to community college for a year or two before you're psychologically ready to go away from home and transfer to a four-year university, so be it. Nothing is more important than your health. Any friendship, relationship, responsibility, or employer that isn't willing to accommodate your health concerns isn't worth your time anyways.

So, if that means putting off preparing for the SAT because you absolutely cannot focus without thinking about the death of a loved one, a recent trauma, or any other affliction, so be it. Don't hold yourself to a standard that forces you to study at the cost of your well-being.

That said, also be honest with yourself. There is a medical difference between sadness and depression, between fear and anxiety, and between a bad day and trauma. Sometimes you just need a pick-me-up. Head over to the library and check out a good self-help book. Watch a comedy. Photograph the sunset. Sing in the shower. Hug your friends tighter. Say "please" and "thank you" for everything and to everyone. Surround yourself with love and with people who inspire you to achieve your dreams.

You should be doing these things regardless of any psychiatric intervention. I remember back in high school so often thinking to myself, "I wish there were just a pill I could take that would make all the pain go away." I grew up in a pretty violent household and had experienced my fair share of trauma, so to add to that the seemingly endless supply of high-school problems was unbearable. My psychiatrist prescribed me Zoloft, and a few weeks later I tried to take my own life. I switched to Prozac, and a few weeks later I attempted suicide again. Short-term, the results were disastrous, but long-term, the medication made a difference: I was absolutely less depressed and never again contemplated self-harm.

I've since come off medication and have never been happier— but the key is that in addition to pharmaceutical help, I made changes in my life. (Have I told you yet that when you get back up after defeat, you have to make changes?) I started exercising, eating better, appreciating small miracles, respecting others, accepting and seeking help when I needed it, and working hard toward my goals. If you'd have told me even two years ago that today I'd be running a bustling online tutoring business and would be publishing my first book, I'd have called you crazy.

Does that mean that just because I made changes that were helpful to me that I expect everyone who's ever suffered through depression will also be able to come out of it? Not necessarily. That said, I have a long family history of depression, anxiety, and bipolar disorder, and I indubitably have a far-lower-than-average potential happiness range. There have been times when I've told myself I'd be forever alone and depressed. During those times, I was alone and depressed. But I've also at times (today included) told myself that I have a great support system and have so much to be thankful for. During those times, I've been far happier and much more productive.

So, here's the dealio: if you need help, seek help, and be honest and reasonable with what you expect from yourself. You can only do so much, and you have to work within your potential. But, no matter what comes your way, take actions that improve your well-being. If that means nixing your SAT prep regimen, then nix your SAT prep regimen.

On the next page is a smattering of recommended reading for those of you who are really going through it:

- *Option B* (Sandberg)
- *On Grief and Grieving* (Kübler-Ross)
- *When Breath Becomes Air* (Kalanithi)
- *You Are A Badass* (Sincero)

Reading from others who have gone through similar traumatic experiences and have come out of them can be super empowering. You are never alone, and there are plenty of people who understand your story and are willing to listen. Let them into your life.

I get a high score on practice exams,
but I don't do nearly as well on the real test.

I'm always surprised that students are surprised when they underperform on exam day. I mean, did you think you were gonna be *less* nervous on the real thing? As always, make sure to mimic real test conditions when you take practice exams (see Page 82). Also, accept that if you generally struggle with focus or anxiety, then you'll probably get a lower score on the real exam than on your practice exams. The stress is higher when you know your score officially counts.

Take deep breaths, relax, wear comfortable clothes, and be aware of whether you'll have more opportunities to take the exam in the future. If taking the exam more than once (or even the first time) will put a financial strain on your family, then see if you can obtain an SAT Fee Waiver to relieve that burden and give you the assurance that you'll be able to take the exam again without forcing your parents into economic strife. Visit www.sat.org/fee-waiver for more information.

You may want to view your first real exam as a "practice real exam." No matter how hard you try, it's impossible to perfectly mimic test-day conditions when you're practicing. Once you've taken a real exam, you know exactly how you perform on test day and can even more accurately adapt your prep regimen to compensate.

Will my score get me into the college I want to attend?
(Or: Is my score high enough yet?)

It might. As I've said before, if you neglect your GPA and hope that your SAT will save you, then you're misguided. GPA is king, so prioritize your coursework. Some students think that a 1600 will get them into any school of their choice. That's not true. Do more students who

> *As soon as you decide you've done "good enough," you close yourself off to improvement.*

score a 1600 get into top colleges than do students who score a 1400? Yes, of course, but that's because the type of student who works hard enough to get a 1600 is also the type of student who works hard enough to get a 4.0 as well. As always, be reasonable with your expectations.

That said, your SAT is a large part (not the largest, but still a large part) of your college application. It's a quick and easy way for colleges to rank applicants, and you should strive to get the highest score that you can. Oh, the number of hours students have wasted over the years by asking people on Reddit and College Confidential to "chance me" given their scores. Instead of brooding in fear about your qualifications, work hard and do the best you can. Shine wherever possible, and don't worry about whether you've surpassed some nonexistent threshold between you and your dreams. Find a new volunteer opportunity, search for an internship, join a new club, or work smarter to improve your score.

As soon as you decide you've done "good enough," you close yourself off to improvement. Never stop improving. I heard something recently that had never occurred to me. Conventional wisdom is that, when auditioning for a talent show like *America's Got Talent* or *The Voice*, you should sandbag—or, start out good so the audience will later be blown away by your great. In other words, you don't want to peak too early. Call it, if you will, the "tip of the iceberg" outlook. I'll just give you the tip of the iceberg for now, but later you'll get the whole thing. (To its credit, the outlook did, after all, bring down the "unsinkable" Titanic.)

But here's the thing: what happens after you've revealed your whole iceberg? Maybe you've maxed out on chainsaws you can juggle or high notes you can sing. Now what? If you get eliminated, then your response is the dreadfully stunting "My best wasn't good enough." When you decide ahead of time what your best is, you don't see new possibilities, and you altogether prevent yourself from improving or pushing boundaries.

If competitors instead started with their best, they'd have no choice but to push themselves toward even bigger and even better. Don't set limits, and always look for ways to improve. I'm not saying to aim for 1700, but I am saying that if you score 1600 on practice tests, don't assume you'll score 1600 on the real exam. You might still have room to grow as a test-taker, and you'll always have room to grow as a student.

Can I reach my SAT goals?

Oh, this is an easy one! Yes, yes, yes, a million times yes! There's nothing you can't achieve with hard work! Okay, maybe if you're 6'4" you'll never be a gymnast, but you get my point. The only thing holding you back is how much time and effort you're willing to seriously invest in improving your score. You will get lost, feel helpless and confused, and feel like you're not improving. That happens to everyone—and any successful person can tell you they've experienced huge setbacks along the path to success. What separates those who achieve from those who don't is perseverance, grit, and the unshakeable confidence that you can achieve it when you believe it.

CHAPTER SIX

Memes Are Your Best Friends

In Chapter Five, as part of my treatment of the "I don't have enough time to study" excuse, I addressed the fact that this meme has infected most students' minds. The single most difficult task I've faced as a tutor and a teacher is convincing students that they have the power to determine their potentials. More tightly than to any other idea do students cling to the notion that they can't change their habits or their abilities. The point of this chapter is to prove to you that you're the boss. *You're in control, and only you get to decide how much you can achieve.* I think that you need to consider the history, behavior, and application of memes if you want to fully appreciate your ability to transform your thinking. Understanding the power of memes is tantamount to understanding the power of your mind. Since the advent of the internet, the word "meme" has been hijacked and redefined beyond its original meaning. In his 1976 book, *The Selfish Gene*, Richard Dawkins coined the term "meme" to refer to self-replicating ideas. When I talk about memes, I'm talking about these Dawkinsonian memes—not pictures of Kermit the Frog drinking Lipton tea. The next three pages might seem a little out-of-place at first. Stick with me. I promise the payoff will be worth the read.

Some history: After the days of Darwin and Mendel, and especially after Watson and Crick's 1953 discovery of the structure of DNA, biologists predominantly concerned themselves with natural selection at the *genetic* level. Genes, the functional units of chromosomal DNA, are basically discrete sets of instructions for making proteins. Some of those proteins are responsible for duplicating DNA, which means that genes are essentially able to copy themselves. Indeed, part of Dawkins's rationale for calling genes "selfish" is that all life more or less exists to copy genes. Everything else—art, music, science, the SAT, this book—is superfluous. The gene is all there is.

This gene-centered point of view permeates psychology, anthropology, ecology, and pretty much all the other -ologies. Why does a certain plant have spiky leaves? Because spiky leaves made its ancestors more likely to survive, meaning they could pass on their genes. Why do humans have emotions? Because emotions made our ancestors more likely to survive, meaning they could pass on their genes. In other words, it's genes all the way down.[1]

That's all well and good, but genetics only goes so far, especially when modern science and medicine can now overcome many genetic disorders and inadequacies. My eyeglasses, for example, allow me to compensate for my genetically-determined poor vision. Out in the wild, I'd be left for dead, but today I fit in just fine, or at least I like to think so.

Eyeglasses aren't genetic, yet they still help genes to survive and replicate. After all, if I can see my environment clearly, then I'm far more likely to survive to reproductive age and have children. There's no gene for eyeglasses, and neither the inventor of eyeglasses nor any optometrists have a special "glasses gene" that everyone else lacks. Where do glasses come from, and why don't tigers and bears have glasses? Why doesn't any other species have science or history or books or video games? What do we have that they don't have? Memes.

Not only does each generation pass on some combination of

---

1 In Douglas Adams's *Hitchhiker's Guide to the Galaxy*, an old woman explains to a scientist that the Earth is really just a plate balanced on the back of a turtle. The scientist inquires what the turtle is standing on, and the woman answers that "it's turtles all the way down." This mimics the theological question, "What created God?"

its genes to the next generation, but it also hands down its knowledge and ideas. Isaac Newton conducted extensive research into the behavior of light, especially as it passes through lenses. His work forms the basis for most modern optics and is partly responsible for my ability to see. Newton didn't pass on his knowledge through genes (most historians agree he likely never had sex). He passed on his knowledge through memes. He published books, gave lectures, and wrote letters. Through the gift of language, his ideas have spread, morphed, and migrated into the minds of physics students the world over for centuries.

But just as no babies are born reading Shakespeare, no babies emerge from the womb solving optics problems either, even if their parents are physicists. Nor, for that matter, does any human baby know how to swim, find its own food, or form shelter. We have very little genetically-programmed ability to do much of anything. Newborn humans are notoriously inept and unable to survive on their own, and yet our species has dominated the globe for millennia. How? Memes.

What we lack in instinct we make up for with ingenuity and creativity. More importantly, once we discover new information or solve new problems, we can spread our discoveries through speech, text, or demonstration. Over generations, our species becomes more competent and able to solve increasingly intricate puzzles. Culture, language, and critical thinking, then, are vital to our success: imagine an isolated group of a hundred or so babies with no access to language or adult influence. They'd be doomed. Our existence depends on the strength and fecundity of our memes.

This is the first point I want to make in this short, final chapter: our success depends on the spread of memes. Just like genes, memes can also self-replicate, as once someone has an idea, then that someone can transmit it to others, and often the collective benefits as a result (think, for instance, of the "how to create fire" meme).

The second point I want to make will affect you much more than the recognition that we rely on our ideas. Do recognize that our ideas need not reflect reality, and they also need not benefit us. Furthermore, the meme pool—the aggregate of all memes that are currently shuffling around between humans—is in constant flux, with some old ideas dying out and other, new ideas joining the fray. Put another way, the current body of human knowledge is only a fraction of all that can be known or understood, and your own personal meme pool is an even smaller fraction thereof. Taken together, these ideas should inspire you immensely.

We grow up with the notion that adults know best and that everything we are taught is accurate. As we grow even older, we begin to realize that a lot of the ideas we've learned are actually inaccurate and sometimes intentionally fictitious, as is the case with propaganda, for example. We almost universally acknowledge that bad ideas exist, but we also nearly all think that our own ideas are totally correct. Like a virus, once a meme latches onto you, it's very tough to get rid of it. Indeed, it sometimes takes superhuman effort to convince yourself that your ideas are wrong. Moreover, our confidence in our beliefs doesn't necessarily reflect the accuracy of those beliefs: you can be completely certain about something that is in actuality false. Our memes can be wrong.

Memes can also hurt us. From a biological perspective, so long as the net total effect of our memes is beneficial, then we are memetically fit. Put another way, if our memes aren't so bad that they kill us, then our memes survive as we do; so long as there are enough positive memes to counteract the negative ones, our species will persist.

We create our own realities.

Negative memes are not only allowable but also widespread. Ideas such as "violence solves problems" and "being rich makes you evil" have plagued societies for centuries. You, too, have likely suffered at the hands of bad memes like "I'm not good enough," which keeps you from putting effort into difficult tasks. Our memes can be harmful.

Finally, just because we lack a meme doesn't mean the underlying truth of that meme doesn't exist. Plate tectonics, as a trite example, existed long before any human word or idea for the concept ever did. We constantly learn new information and make new discoveries, but that doesn't mean that that information and those discoveries didn't exist before we acquired the memes for them. Similarly, just because we hold untrue or negative ideas doesn't make them true or positive; just because they're *our* memes doesn't mean they're right. That said, our memes are flexible, and our ideas can adapt to new information, different cultures, and varied experiences. What you believe about the world today is likely very different from what you believed a decade ago—and it's likely very different from what you'll believe in another decade. Our memes are plastic.

What this means is that we create our own realities. Our perception of ourselves and our world is the sum of our memes, which we have the power to change. You have the power to determine your potential. You can replace bad memes with good ones, wrong ones with right ones. If your parents, teachers, siblings, or anyone else, yourself included, has convinced you that you're dumb, untalented, boring, lame, or unlikely to succeed, then you can change that. Those are just memes. Those memes are wrong, harmful, and mutable.

Now, that's not to say that changing your mind can get you out of any predicament. Simply telling yourself "I'm going to get an A on my math test" or "I'm going to get up on time" won't accomplish much on its own. Should you decide to not study for your test or to stay in bed all day, then your fate is sealed. But, why do you make those *decisions* in the first place? Memes.

What might keep you from studying? Maybe you think that you'll fail no matter how hard you try. That's just a meme, likely reinforced by some combination of past poor performance, disdain for your teacher, and a general lack of interest in academia. If you're to have any chance convincing yourself to study and get a good grade, then you have to change your foundational ideas about your abilities. You make decisions based on your beliefs, so when your beliefs are bad, your actions are, too.

To change your beliefs, you have to first truly accept that your beliefs can be wrong—and then that they are wrong. Most of us agree that we've been wrong but think that we aren't wrong anymore. We are. You are. Much of what I think is true is actually false, and much of what you believe is reality is complete nonsense. Presidents, religious leaders, teachers, professors, parents, friends, neighbors, and even Einstein himself have all been wrong about an uncountable number of things, and they will all continue to be wrong. Our memes are fallible, and that's okay. Misconception is a part of existence.

The most important piece of this meme puzzle is that you and your ideas are not the same thing. Memes are parasitic; you can survive just fine without most of them, but they're hopeless without you. You have all the power. You're the host, and you get to decide which memes you want to kick out of your life and which ones you want to keep. Therefore, it's impossible to make accurate "I am" statements. You're not anything. At every point, you get to decide how you want to act, think, and be. You're the boss. Our tendency to define and create permanent identities for ourselves and others is intellectually bankrupt; we should know better, and we're capable of better.

> *We should define ourselves by our potentials.*

We should define ourselves by our potentials. Perhaps you lack a skill or competency today. I, for instance, have never once practiced or learned how to dance, but that doesn't mean that I was born with or am permanently stuck with an inability to dance. With proper practice, I very well could become an amazing dancer. The potential is there; I've just decided to not tap into it. That outlook gives me power, and it gives me options. There's tremendous daylight between "I'm a bad dancer" and "I haven't trained at dancing." The former consigns and relegates you, telling you that you're not a good dancer because you weren't *born* a good dancer—ignoring, by the way, the overwhelming amount of time that great dancers have invested in their craft. The latter empowers you with the ability to choose what you want to be and do. Memes are powerful, and the way you speak and think about yourself determines what you can accomplish. It's no coincidence that the word "potential" derives from the Latin word "*potens*," which means "powerful." Your power *is* your potential, and don't you ever forget it.

All in all, the memes that you choose to believe, adhere to, abide by, and repeat to yourself will dictate your success. You likely have a very discerning sense for which memes are harmful—say, "School is for losers!"—and which memes are beneficial—say, "Knowledge is power!" Kick the bad ones to the curb. Sometimes that's hard to do. Do it. Make it happen. You're better than letting lame memes control your accomplishments. Stop yourself every time you start spouting falsehoods like "I'm bad at math" or "The SAT is too hard for me." Are you stuck in a permanent state of inability, or do you have control over what you can achieve? (In case the answer isn't clear: you have the power!)

Bad memes are at the heart of the SAT reading epidemic, and good memes are at the heart of your perfect score. Think of it this way: everyone who's ever told you that you're not capable of anything you put your mind to was just infected by bad ideas. They succumbed to lame memes and couldn't see potential. If you accept that your potential is just as vast as anyone else's, then there's nothing you can't do. Unleash your inner awesome, put in the work, and don't let anything get in your way. You can unlearn everything your teachers taught you, and you can get a perfect score.

APPENDIX

As you're reading passages to practice for the SAT, you need to remain cognizant of *why* you're reading. What are you looking for? What information is important? What questions do you need to be able to answer when you're finished reading a text? For this reason, I have provided this appendix of four worksheets to guide your practice. You don't need to actually write down any answers to these questions, but, should you choose do so, don't waste your time writing complete sentences. Work smarter, not harder. Doing more isn't always doing more. That said, you do need to *answer* each of the questions if you want to be sure you're both properly understanding your readings and focusing on relevant details. You don't need a giant workbook. You just need these.

These worksheet questions, plus some bonus questions, are also available on my website, www.tutorjacob.com, under the Books tab. Save these pdfs to your phone or computer and print them out so you'll always have them, even when you don't have this book on-hand. Feel free to tear out these pages. The long-term goal is for you to have these guiding questions on your mind whenever you engage with texts. When you're a more active reader, you're better able to understand, interpret, and respond to others' arguments and ideas. These are the abilities that the SAT reading exam tests. If you want a perfect score, then prioritize developing these skills, and keep the following questions with you always.

Straight Up Literature

Vocabulary + Structure

- Did you encounter any new words? Write them down and learn them.
- Does the author italicize, bolden, or repeat any text? What effect does this emphasis have?
- Does the author put quotes around any words or phrases? Why?
- Did you find any confusing or awkward sentence structures? Can you understand what the author was saying?

Plot

- What was the primary conflict between characters, within a character, or between a character and the setting?
- What were the most important details and interactions? Why did they stand out? How do they fit into the narrative overall?
- Is the focus of the narrative consistent, or does it shift?
- If the focus shifts, how do the different points of focus relate to each other? Does one story or point of focus introduce you to another?

Analysis

- Can you identify how the characters feel about each other or about themselves?
- What textual evidence allows you to identify those feelings?
- What mood does the setting create?
- Does any dialogue or description of the setting foreshadow later events?
- From what point of view is the story told? Why do you think the author chose this point of view?
- Does the point of view change over the course of the story? If so, what effect does this have?

Old People Talking About Politics and Society

Vocabulary + Structure

- Did you encounter any new words? Are they specific to this time period? Write them down and learn them.
- Does the author italicize, bolden, or repeat any text? Why?
- Does the author put quotes around any words or phrases? Why?
- Did you find any confusing or awkward sentence structures? Can you understand what the author was saying?
- How does the author's style compare to other authors' styles?

Argument

- What is the author's principal argument?
- What evidence does the author present to support this argument?
- How does the author address counterarguments? Does the author make any concessions?
- Does the author make any assumptions? How do we know they're assumptions and not facts?
- How does this author's argument compare to other arguments you've read, either from the same or a different time period?

Author + Audience Analysis

- How does the author establish the significance of his/her argument? Whom does the issue affect?
- Does the author have a personal stake in the argument?
- To whom is the author writing or speaking? Is the author trying to change public opinion? To spark political action?
- What is the author's tone? Is the author fervent, worried, reserved, or somewhere in between? What evidence supports this?
- What are this author's core beliefs? What are some ideas with which, based on textual evidence, you could be sure the author agrees?

New People Talking About Politics and Society

Vocabulary + Structure

- Did you encounter any new words? Are they specific to this time period? Write them down and learn them.
- Does the author italicize, bolden, or repeat any text? Why?
- Does the author put quotes around any words or phrases? Why?
- Did you find any confusing or awkward sentence structures? Can you understand what the author was saying?
- How does the author's style compare to other authors' styles?

Argument

- What is the author's principal argument? With what evidence?
- How does the author address counterarguments? Does the author make any concessions?
- Does the author make any assumptions? How do we know they're assumptions and not facts?
- Does the author provide data? How do the data support the author's argument? Read any graphs very carefully.
- How does this author's argument compare to other arguments you've read, either from the same or a different time period?

Author + Audience Analysis

- How does the author establish the significance of his/her argument? Whom does the issue affect?
- Does the author have a personal stake in the argument?
- To whom is the author writing or speaking? Is the author trying to change public opinion? To spark political action?
- What is the author's tone? Is the author fervent, worried, reserved, or somewhere in between? What evidence supports this?
- What are this author's core beliefs? What are some ideas with which, based on evidence, you could be sure the author agrees?

(Social) Science Experiments and Summaries

Vocabulary + Structure
- Did you encounter any new words? Are they specific to this particular field of research? Write them down and learn them.
- Does the author italicize, bolden, or quote any text? Why?
- Is this a primary source or a secondary source? Is the author making an argument or reporting on research?

Significance
- What experiments led the researchers to conduct this inquiry? Did these lead the researchers to make any assumptions?
- Did the results of the experiment inspire further research?
- How are the results of the research medically, socially, or economically relevant? What's the significance of the research?
- Does the author discuss the future of this field of research? Is this a brand new field, or is this research in a well-established field?

Experimental Analysis
- Who conducted the experiment(s)? If there were multiple, were they connected? Did the results of one inspire another?
- What methods/procedures did the experimenters follow? What were their control, independent, and dependent variable(s)?
- How did the design of the experiment(s) relate to any hypotheses the researchers had? In other words, *why* did the researchers choose that design?
- What were the experimental results? Are they consistent with any hypotheses? Are the results quantitative or qualitative? Are they displayed in a figure?
- Does the author present any conclusions as conjectures? As irrefutable facts? What words does the author use to make this clear?

Made in United States
Orlando, FL
24 January 2022

13987603R00086